Praise for

Imagine a future in which t
customers. No management. No administrators. No
middle layers at all. Imagine a future in which the tools
you use get smarter every time you make an error—and
pass that knowledge along to the same tools other people
are using around the world. Imagine a future where data
is so vast and so cheap that the rate of innovation we see
today will seem glacial by comparison. That's a picture of
the future Patrick Schwerdtfeger masterfully assembles
from data, trends and case studies in *Anarchy, Inc.*, and
it's a provocative mosaic I can't get out of my head.

It's a future in which the haves and have-nots will grow
further apart, but the potential for society as a whole
to thrive reaches unprecedented heights. It's a future in
which some of the most basic systems and ideas driving
business today will be replaced with radically different
approaches. It's a future rooted in anarchy—not the dark,
simplistic and dystopic anarchy of sci-fi novels, but the
inevitable and empowering anarchy of a cultural shift
away from centralized services and toward exponential
individual opportunity.

John Armato, Senior Partner &
Creative Strategist, FleishmanHillard

Patrick Schwerdtfeger's *Anarchy, Inc.* provides predictive
models and highly effective tools that will enable CEO's
to thrive in an increasingly disruptive world.

Craig Hettrich, President of Renaissance Executive
Forums, Former CEO of Java City

Profiting in the new economy will take vision, boldness, and knowledge which is why *Anarchy, Inc.* is a must-read for the leaders of today . . . and tomorrow!

Jerry Ross, President, National Entrepreneur Center

Do you embrace disruption or ignore it? Patrick Schwerdtfeger's book *Anarchy, Inc.* gives insights on how to embrace not only blockchain and AI, but the global implications that will impact us all. If you want to find a way to embrace the disruption while being self-reliant, this is the book for you.

John Livesay, CMO, Quantm.one, Author of *The Successful Pitch*

Schwerdtfeger's *Anarchy, Inc.* is as close as it gets to predicting the future and is a must read! If you don't believe society is in the middle of a revolution, this book will convince you otherwise. The content is sure to engage busy executives around the water cooler and stimulate new ways to approach strategy in an increasingly decentralized and disruptive world. If you want to be a business leader and be ahead of the competition, read this book!

John G. Wensveen, PhD, Vice Provost, Miami Dade College

Patrick presents the argument that we can thrive amidst anarchy; that we need to think about our industry and stay on offense. We must run towards innovation, planning carefully when to invest in new technologies. This is a 'must read' for every professional looking to sustain and grow his business and advise his clients through the coming revolution.

Jon Lisby, Chief Executive Officer, Kreston International Ltd.

ANARCHY, INC.

BY PATRICK
SCHWERDTFEGER

ANARCHY, INC.

PROFITING IN A DECENTRALIZED WORLD WITH ARTIFICIAL INTELLIGENCE AND BLOCKCHAIN

BY PATRICK SCHWERDTFEGER

Copyright © 2018 by Patrick Schwerdtfeger. All rights reserved.

No part of this publication may be reproduced, stored in a retrieval system, or transmitted in any form or by any means, electronic, mechanical, photocopying, recording, scanning, or otherwise, without the prior written permission of the author.

Limit of Liability/Disclaimer of Warranty: While the publisher and author have used their best efforts in preparing this book, they make no representations or warranties with respect to the accuracy or completeness of the contents of this book and specifically disclaim any implied warranties of merchantability or fitness for a particular purpose. No warranty may be created or extended by sales representatives or written sales materials. The advice and strategies contained herein may not be suitable for your situation. You should consult with a professional when appropriate. Neither the publisher nor the author shall be liable for any loss of profit or any other commercial damages, including but not limited to special, incidental, consequential, personal, or other damages.

Anarchy, Inc.
Profiting in a Decentralized World with
Artificial Intelligence and Blockchain

By Patrick Schwerdtfeger

1. BUS086000 2. BUS073000 3. BUS020000

ISBN: 978-1-935953-92-0

Cover design by Lewis Agrell

Printed in the United States of America

Authority Publishing
11230 Gold Express Dr. #310-413
Gold River, CA 95670
800-877-1097
www.AuthorityPublishing.com

In memory of
Bryan Beyer.
(1967–2018)

I wish you were
still with us.

ACKNOWLEDGEMENTS

Many people had a direct impact on this book. First and foremost, John Armato provided invaluable insights and feedback. He spent an entire day with me, reviewing models of innovation and strategic questions worth considering, and provided specific guidance on this manuscript as well. You have a brilliant mind, John. Thank you for sharing your creative genius with me.

Karla Nelson, you're a rainmaker. I've never met someone who leads with generosity as consistently as you. Thank you for all the introductions and connections, delivered on a silver platter, as usual. Your approach to business (and to life in general) is inspiring.

Allen Fahden, the cover of this book is your brainchild. Your creativity is unmatched. You helped me with my

TED Talk speech concept, and you've helped me again with this book project. I'm delighted to work with you and Karla to deliver innovation training to our clients.

Judy Robinett, thank you for writing the foreword for this book. It was serendipitous to meet you in the lobby of the Grand America Hotel in Salt Lake City all those years ago. I am one of your biggest fans. Your vision and perspective are always thought provoking.

Rob Ludlow, you were the first one to provide comments and suggestions. Thank you for being so thorough with your edits, and for providing so many other resources along the way. Your willingness to dig into the topic and explore competing narratives is unique.

Annette Schwerdtfeger, my big sister, you edited this manuscript just as you did with my last title. I never expected you to take such an active role in my book projects. You consistently notice mistakes that others miss. Thank you for taking the time to read my work and provide such detailed feedback.

Leslie Eisenberg, you were another unexpected contributor. With only four days' notice, you provided over twenty pages of notes, suggestions, and corrections. I'm grateful for your curiosity and your near-immediate turnaround.

Stephanie Chandler, this is the second book you have published for me. Your counsel and direction are invaluable. Thanks for your recommendations and also for your patience. Writing books wouldn't be as much fun without your input.

Tom Bentley, you are an editing aficionado. I'm so happy that Stephanie introduced you to me. Thanks for your thoughtful and detailed edits, not only on this title but also on *Keynote Mastery* two years ago.

Tom Loarie, you've been a mentor to me since 2009. Our lunches at Pete's Brass Rail are always a pleasure. Your concern, example, and guidance challenge me to become a better person. Thank you for reading and reviewing my books.

Omaid Homayun, thank you for connecting me with some of the brilliant people in your world. You've supported my work for years, providing insights on obscure topics and emerging trends. Those insights inevitably found their way into this book.

Other suggestions and edits came from Andrew McCririck, Cathleen Hoffman, David Chen, Jim Geraghty, John Wensveen, Jon Lisby, Kathy Alice Brown, Kevin Nothstine, Luanne Stevensen, Michael Kongo, Mukund Ghangurde, and Dr. Patti Fletcher. I am grateful for your contributions.

CONTENTS

FOREWORD
(BY JUDY ROBINETT)

If you've been watching the news, you're already well aware of the amazing disruptive technologies that are blindsiding the business world. Artificial intelligence, virtual/augmented reality, blockchain, and initial coin offerings (ICOs) are now affecting every industry sector.

Blockchain is touted as a bigger idea than the Internet itself. And as Patrick points out, the banking industry knows disruption is coming. They're investing heavily to avoid becoming the next dinosaur. Banking isn't the only industry either. Law enforcement, real estate, shipping and distribution, ride-hailing, and many others could also have blockchain in their future.

Last year when I was at NASA, I asked one of the directors if he would've ever guessed that Jeff Bezos, founder and CEO of Amazon, and Elon Musk, founder and

CEO of Tesla, would be launching rockets! They never saw it coming. What else is coming? How will these developments affect you and your business? If you're lucky enough to read this book, you'll soon find out.

Patrick's book *Anarchy, Inc.* holds the answers. Better still, it'll help you learn how to anticipate future trends while they're just on the bleeding edge of technology, allowing you to capture opportunities before the crowd.

The reason I love this book is that it's filled with rich examples showcasing how disruptive technologies, demographic trends, and the "think bigger" mindset are radically changing our world. Imagine how you or your business might prosper from this knowledge. While many people are predicting massive job layoffs and pending doom from a decentralized world, the truth is that the downside is much smaller than the tremendous upside.

Think about the difference between those who are excited and those who are afraid. Those who approach the future with excitement are playing offense, positioning themselves for opportunity. Those who approach the future with fear are playing defense, worrying that new business models will displace their own.

From a private equity standpoint, in a rapidly approaching future, we need to find entrepreneurs who are playing offense. We need to find those who are positioning themselves for the future. The opportunity for profit is enormous. This book will help you claim your share.

Anarchy, Inc. is the perfect guidebook for playing offense. It provides a highly insightful discussion of the technologies reshaping our world, and the impact they will have on everyone. While there are plenty of risks to worry about, there are also countless opportunities to be excited about; opportunities that have never been possible until today. This book focuses on those opportunities.

There has never been a better time to be an entrepreneur. Development costs for technology solutions are a fraction of historical equivalents. Investment capital has never been more abundant. This book provides strategic direction for entrepreneurs, business executives, and investors who want to profit from emerging opportunities.

Judy Robinett, author of
How to Be a Power Connector
(McGraw Hill, 2014)

INTRODUCTION
ANARCHY IS COMING.
WILL YOU BE READY?

CHANGE IS COMING.

Decentralization has already planted its roots.

Anarchy is within sight. In fact, elements of anarchy are already here.

A few will flourish while the majority struggle. This book will help you to be among the winners, not the losers.

There's a revolution taking place right now, and most people aren't even aware of it. Of those that are, very few comprehend the degree of disruption on the horizon. Technology is redefining every corner of our world, and it's evolving along an exponential curve. The impacts will shake humanity to its core. Tomorrow's leaders need to understand the trends and causal relationships to succeed, they need to understand the dynamics of disruptive innovation, and they need to recognize the implications of an increasingly decentralized world.

This book provides models and frameworks for understanding the future. It provides strategic questions to navigate both threats and opportunities. It provides tools to anticipate disruptive innovation, regardless of the industry in question. This book helps leaders predict and dominate tomorrow's economy.

To be clear, the impacts of technology are both positive and negative. Countless things will improve. Indeed, *we are optimizing our planet.* Company by company, region by region, country by country, we are optimizing absolutely everything. Operations are becoming more efficient. Products and services are becoming more intuitive and integrated. The world is becoming more intelligent.

But there are also negative impacts on the way. *Dramatic increases in productivity will diminish the value of human capital.* Algorithms and robotics will displace literally hundreds of millions of jobs. Meanwhile, technology is enabling a shift from centralized power structures to decentralized power structures. The combination is fueling an increasingly individualistic, tribal, and self-reliant world. It's leading to anarchy on a global scale.

The implications are vast, and we have a lot to cover. Let's get started.

Enabling Anarchy

What is anarchy? Is it a world where hoodie-wearing hackers control the Internet? Does it involve chaos and violent street riots? Will that world be ruled by criminal gangs and liberty-seeking armed militias? No, not necessarily. Anarchy refers to a society that rejects power—nothing more, nothing less. It's a political philosophy that advocates self-governance, liberty, and fierce independence.

There are a number of trends that are pushing our society toward anarchy. This book describes those trends and highlights emerging business opportunities for CEOs, founders, executives, and investors. The book covers six broad trends, all converging and overlapping with each other. Anarchy is one of those trends.

Section One looks at the collapsing cost structure of data: the linchpin of the entire technology revolution. With costs plummeting and capabilities skyrocketing, businesses are reshaping one industry after another.

Section Two dives into artificial intelligence: the ultimate use case for data. Technology is climbing a ladder of complexity. Artificial intelligence implies complexity requiring human-level comprehension, and milestones are being achieved at an accelerating rate.

Section Three addresses the imminent job losses we can expect at the hands of algorithms, robotics, and artificial intelligence. Massive job displacement by automation will bring anger to our citizens and chaos to our political system, sowing the seeds of anarchy.

Section Four introduces blockchain and the exploding world of cryptocurrencies. Blockchain protocol enables peer-to-peer transactions between non-trusting parties, requiring no central governing authority. Blockchain enables decentralization, and decentralization enables anarchy.

Section Five pulls these trends together. Massive job losses and technology-enabled decentralization are ushering in a wholesale cultural shift that values liberty, self-reliance, and individualism above all else. Anarchy is coming. Will you be ready?

Section Six describes the relationship between demographics, economic growth, and entrepreneurialism. Demographic data is a major contributor to long-term economic forecasting. It may not be directly related to technology, but its impact on economic activity is impossible to ignore.

Today's leaders are woefully unprepared for tomorrow's opportunities and challenges. Disruptive innovation regularly catches intelligent and accomplished executives off guard, and anarchy is a form of disruption. It explains many of the cultural changes we're already living with today, but we're just getting started. There's a tsunami of change on the way.

This tsunami spells trouble for many, but that's not the focus of this book. Instead, *Anarchy, Inc.* highlights the exciting technologies and unprecedented business opportunities waiting to be exploited. These are transformative times, and you're in the right place at the right time. Grab your surfboard. We're gonna ride this one in!

SECTION ONE: DATA
WHEN COSTS COLLAPSE, INNOVATION THRIVES

The fundamental ingredient in modern technology is data. Data processing, data bandwidth, and data storage form the backbone of all digital technologies. Over the past sixty years, the cost structure of that processing, bandwidth, and storage has collapsed. Let's look at data storage. In particular, let's look at the cost of storing one terabyte of data. Just to review:

1,000 bytes = 1 kilobyte (KB)

1,000 KB = 1 megabyte (MB)

1,000 MB = 1 gigabyte (GB)

1,000 GB = 1 terabyte (TB)

In 2000, the cost of storing one terabyte of data was about $17,000. In 2020, the cost is anticipated to be just

$3 for the exact same thing (Amazon S3 "glacier storage" pricing was $4/TB in 2018). Think about that. In just twenty years, the cost will have dropped by 99.98%. And it's not just happening in data storage. The same thing is happening in data bandwidth and data processing.

That's the nature of exponential growth. Technology is evolving along an exponential curve. When people think about exponential curves, they automatically think about the hockey stick curve that launches practically vertical on the right-hand side of the graph, and that's exactly what the line does. The capabilities explode over time. But the inverse is that the cost of any one capability plummets.

That's what's happening in the data space. Costs are plummeting. Everything involving data is becoming cheaper—quickly! *Everybody* is going to be in the data business in the future. What would happen in your industry if all of your competitors were fully leveraging data in their businesses? Today, it might still be a competitive advantage to be data-driven. Tomorrow, it will be a competitive disadvantage *not* to be.

Exponential Thinking

Business leaders need to think exponentially. Unfortunately, humans are hardwired to think in linear terms. That's our instinct. It's unnatural to think in exponential terms. The numbers expand too quickly after a while. The growth seems impossible.

There's a parable of an Indian ruler who wanted to reward a wise man who invented the game of chess. The wise man could pick a reward of his choosing. He requested one grain of rice for the first square of the chessboard, two grains of rice on the second, four on the third, eight on the fourth, and doubling on each square thereafter. Initially, it seems quite reasonable. But after about half the board, the numbers start multiplying at an insane pace. By the last square, the wise man would receive more rice than the country's entire annual harvest.

Another classic example of exponential growth involves lily pads growing on a pond. Every day, the number of lily pads doubles. On the 30th day, the pond is 100% covered by lily pads. The question is: When was it just 50% covered?

The answer is the 29th day. If the number of lily pads doubles each day, and the pond is completely covered on the 30th day, it would be only 50% covered on the 29th day, one day earlier. It seems counterintuitive at first, but it makes perfect sense when thinking exponentially.

That's what business leaders need to do. It's not natural. You literally need to coach yourself to think exponentially. I do that myself. Exponential thinking can be learned. It's like a muscle. You get better at it with practice. Make it an essential part of each day. Remind yourself constantly to think in exponential terms.

What could you do if your analytics were 10 times more powerful than they are today?

What could you do if the software was 1/10th the price that it is today?

Who would invest in this technology if it cost 1/100th of the current price?

The Human Genome Project, started in 1990, is one of the best real-life examples of exponential progress. By 1997, seven years after the project began, they had only completed 1% of the job. With that announcement, many scientists assumed they'd need another 700 years to finish the project. But of course, that's not what happened. There were a few people who understood that at the time.

Ray Kurzweil, author of among others *The Singularity Is Near*, founder of Singularity University and Director of Engineering at Google, is well known for thinking exponentially. He's been predicting the future for decades with remarkable success, and he looked at the genome situation very differently. He said, "If we're at 1%, we're almost done." Think about that! "If we're at 1%, we're halfway there." From a linear perspective, it seems impossible. But exponentially, it makes sense.

If something is scaling at 100% per year (in other words, it's doubling every year), how many years does it take to get from 1% to 100%? The answer is about six and a half years. In the first year, 1% goes to 2%. In the second, 2% goes to 4%, then 8%, then 16%, then 32%, and then 64%. That's the sixth year. So in the seventh year, you pop up over 100%. In an exponential environment, progress happens quickly!

That's exactly what happened. The project was completed in April 2003, slightly ahead of that schedule. Since then, the cost of sequencing the human genome has dropped from $2.7 billion to under $1,000 today. Raymond McCauley, Chair of Digital Biology at Singularity University, believes it'll cost just pennies by 2020. That's the power of exponential growth.

Solar power is another area that's evolving along an exponential curve. It's not scaling at 100% per year. Instead, it's been scaling at about 25% per year recently. But at that rate, with global energy consumption growing at about 1.8% per year, solar power could supply global demand as early as 2041.

We don't yet know if those trends will continue into the future. There are lots of variables involved. But if the current growth rates continue, solar power could play a dominant role in the global energy mix within twenty years, and that's regardless of who's in the White House. Technology is completely independent of politics. When looking at a chart of technological innovation, major political events (like the Vietnam War, 9/11, or the 2008 financial crisis) have almost no impact at all. Technology continues to evolve either way.

Innovation = f(Capabilities)

Innovation is a function of capabilities. As capabilities increase, opportunistic businesses fill the gap with better and more powerful services. YouTube and other video services emerged when data-bandwidth capabilities made online video streaming possible. Countless mobile apps emerged after the iPhone was launched along with the App Store.

This reality—that innovation is a function of capabilities—makes it possible to anticipate the future. The capabilities in data have been remarkably predictable for the past sixty years. If data processing, bandwidth, and storage can be projected into the future, you can start to imagine what new services would logically be introduced along the way.

Moore's Law predicts that the number of transistors on an integrated circuit doubles approximately every two years. That term was coined in 1965 and it's been chugging along ever since. Today, we're nearing the end of the current paradigm of microchip development. Transistors are currently just fourteen nanometers across, smaller than most viruses. You can't get much smaller than that. But that obstacle will only lead to new paradigms in the future.

Already today, semiconductor companies are exploiting 3D chip designs and using graphic processing units (GPUs) rather than central processing units (CPUs) because they're better suited to today's machine learning algorithms. Google has now developed their own chips (called Tensor Processing Units or TPUs) specifically designed to work well with their TensorFlow machine learning framework, resulting in a 15x to 30x performance improvement over traditional GPUs ("In-Datacenter Performance Analysis of a Tensor Processing Unit™," Google, Inc., June 26, 2017). The increases in overall chip performance continue to evolve.

Then there's quantum computing. Although the technology is far from proven, companies including D-Wave, IBM, and Google are pioneering research that would increase processing power by 1,000-fold or more, possibly *much* more. If quantum computing is ever perfected, it would represent a gigantic leap in capabilities in a single step.

The point is that capabilities continue to increase, so innovation will continue as well. What would be possible in your industry if data processing was 100 times faster than it is today? What about data bandwidth or data storage? Who would use the technology if it became ten times cheaper? These milestones will all be reached in the not-so-distant future.

The role of data in business is increasing all the time. Imagine the most cutting-edge data-driven solutions currently in your industry. Today, those solutions represent a competitive advantage. In five years, every single one of your competitors will be using that same technology. What currently represents a competitive advantage will soon become essential just to survive.

Innovation Propagation

The first people to implement new technology pay the most. It's new. It's unproven. People don't yet know where the return on investment (ROI) will come from. The process involves a lot of trial and error, and that costs money, not to mention the new systems, software development, and implementation costs. It's all very expensive.

In the early days of the "big data" revolution, 2011 and 2012, the ROI of big data initiatives among Fortune 500 companies was mostly negative. They were losing money. They were investing millions but had yet to identify incremental profits. But all those investments—paying for exploratory work, proofs of concept (POCs), pilot programs, and new system implementations—yielded better results in the years that followed.

In terms of use cases, three of the early winners were behavioral targeting (marketing), predictive maintenance (operations), and logistics (distribution). Let's look at each one in turn.

Behavioral targeting is all about understanding customers better. What are their lifestyles like? Besides using your product or service, what else do they like to do? By building a multi-dimensional customer profile, it becomes easier to target them in other settings, but that involves a huge amount of data.

The development of these targeted marketing strategies allowed endless niche markets to be accessed and exploited by data-driven marketers, yielding profits difficult to find using traditional methods. Imagine targeting fly-fishing enthusiasts or victims of identity theft through traditional channels. Both are easy to target online.

On top of that, behavioral targeting made it easier to avoid marketing to the *wrong* people, reducing wasted advertising dollars. Data-driven online marketing delivered measurable ROI. It was an early winner in the big data revolution.

Google AdWords is the perfect example. Small businesses can leverage enormous data to target potential customers at an affordable clip. They can show tailored ads to demographically specific users in geographically specific locations during specific hours when those users search for specific keyword phrases. The targeting is incredible. This would never have been possible before Google's AdWords advertising platform. Today, it's readily available.

Predictive maintenance is about anticipating maintenance requirements before machines actually break. This was another area for quick ROI. When machines break down, it can grind the entire production line to a halt. That costs a lot of money. By avoiding unexpected work stoppages, predictive maintenance was an early winner for big data initiatives.

Logistics was a third area for positive ROI. By optimizing delivery routes, monitoring traffic conditions, and identifying and selling excess capacity, companies were able to squeeze more profit from regular distribution operations.

This can be seen on the airlines. It used to be common to have empty seats on flights. It was rare to have every seat taken. Not anymore! The airlines have become incredibly good at filling their flights. How are they doing it? They're monitoring search activity, ticket sales, and travel trends. They're using dynamic pricing models and adjusting flight schedules. It's all driven by data.

Businesses are using data to optimize the marketing and delivery of their products and services. The situation is different when the data is itself the product. Credit rating agencies such as TransUnion, Equifax, and Experian come to mind. Their product *is* the data, so they were among the first to leverage big data technologies. But for all other companies who were analyzing data to look for new efficiencies, success stories were slower to emerge.

Innovation propagates through use cases and success stories. As the early adopters try new things and eventually identify positive ROI, everyone else follows suit and implements similar systems in their own businesses. The competitive process mandates it. If your competitor exploits new technologies with positive ROI, you have to do the same or lose out in the marketplace.

Before long, enterprise software providers incorporate successful use cases into their platforms. Customer relationship management (CRM) platforms including Salesforce and Zoho contributed to the marketing applications, and enterprise resource planning (ERP) platforms supported the operations applications.

CRM and ERP software platforms then deliver these new capabilities to small and medium-sized enterprises (SME). This is the point when new technologies propagate from the industry giants down to the mid-market players. Of course, as the cost of new technologies come down, so do the associated benefits within the marketplace.

If you're the only one using a new technology in your industry, you enjoy a competitive advantage: a monopolistic position, either attracting new customers or earning outsized margins. But as the technology propagates and all of your competitors start using it too, the advantage erodes and eventually shifts to a disadvantage for those who fail to adopt it themselves.

Think about your industry. You have large competitors—dominant players in your industry—and small competitors. You also have high gross-profit competitors and low gross-profit competitors. Generally speaking, the large and/or high gross-profit competitors will embrace new technologies first. They're the only ones who can afford it. They enjoy the "first-mover advantage," but they pay a high price for it.

Over time, their trial-and-error investments make it cheaper for other companies to follow suit. Adoption works its way down the gross profit ranking until it reaches the small and/or low gross-profit commodity producers.

Keep in mind that gross profit comes from two different business strategies. Some companies have impressive margins built into their pricing strategy. Apple is a great example. They have impressive profit margins.

Other companies sell huge quantities of goods or services at lower margins, but the sheer volume results in significant gross profit anyway. Amazon, Walmart, and Costco are good examples. Their margins are thin, but they sell tons of stuff. This is common in China as well. They want volume! With higher quantities, lower margins still generate sufficient gross profit to innovate early.

For the old industry stalwarts, the greatest obstacle to innovation is often their old legacy systems. This can relegate high gross-profit companies to the bottom of the innovation list. You can't endlessly apply patches on top of outdated legacy software. Eventually, you have to replace the whole system, and that's a daunting task.

Innovation has to come from the top. C-level executives need to drive change if the big investments are to materialize. Legacy systems might be holding the process back. If so, someone with authority has to pull the trigger. Someone has to make change happen. Make note of the companies that have that leadership, and those that do not.

This is a valuable tool to anticipate when investments need to be made. Create a list of your competitors, sorted by gross profit. Think about the newest technologies in your field and who's exploiting them at this stage. In all likelihood, the high gross-profit and progressive players are leading the charge. Previous technologies were probably embraced in the same order, and that order will likely continue into the future.

Having a list of industry participants in order of innovation adoption is extremely useful. Remember, the first ones to embrace new technology pay the most. Costs drop over time. Everybody talks about the first-mover advantage, but there are substantial benefits to the second-mover advantage as well. By monitoring new technology adoption in your industry, you can plan when to invest in new technologies and minimize the cost required.

The Internet of Things (IoT)

The collapsing cost structure in the data space has fueled the entire technological revolution. Data was the first step. Processing, transmitting, and storing data became cheaper and cheaper. As a result, it made economic sense to measure and record more and more data. Businesses started adding sensors to the products they sold. As the volume of sensors increased, their cost naturally dropped, further accelerating the trend.

The term "Internet of Things" (IoT) gained traction in 2013. It refers to the explosion of Internet-connected sensors in devices we use every day. Some call it machine-to-machine (M2M) and there are estimates that we'll have over fifty billion devices connected to the Internet by 2020.

In most cases, these sensors are incorporated into devices by their respective manufacturers. These devices include smartphones, cars, appliances, homes, and buildings, and the resulting data-driven insights are delivered (to both manufacturers and device owners) on mobile apps and other user interfaces.

Jeff Bezos, founder and CEO of Amazon, once said, "The only thing that's disruptive is customer adoption." If people adopt new technology, it becomes disruptive. If they don't, disruption doesn't happen. So, do people use the data-driven insights provided by IoT sensors? Some certainly do, but many do not.

The Industrial Internet of Things (IIoT) refers to the increasing use of sensors in industrial settings. Many industrial machines come fully equipped with sensors, and ERP (enterprise resource planning) providers are adding application programming interfaces (APIs) to allow data to flow directly into their digital systems. Whether or not these capabilities are leveraged is up to the customers. Once again, some certainly do, but many do not.

Make it a priority to exploit the capabilities you already have access to. Data-driven insights are increasingly available from the industrial machines and consumer devices we use. The easiest way to improve performance is to familiarize yourself with the capabilities already available on these devices.

It's always interesting to analyze your industry and see who's exploiting capabilities first. Early adopters generally have support and encouragement from owners and top executives. Map out a path that these innovations normally take in your industry. See who's first and who's last. Where do you sit on that list?

The IoT and IIoT have already had huge implications in manufacturing. I mentioned predictive maintenance earlier. Machines can be outfitted with sensors that measure temperature and vibration, for example, allowing algorithms to anticipate problems before they occur. That allows companies to do maintenance on their own terms and avoid unexpected work stoppages.

Rolls Royce builds the huge jet engines that propel the double-decker Airbus A380 airplane. Those "Trent" engines are outfitted with dozens of sensors, including cameras that operate at 2,000°C while the plane is still in flight, allowing maintenance crews to diagnose problems and proactively service engines before major problems arise.

According to their 2012 annual report, Rolls Royce actually earns more than half of its profits from lucrative maintenance contracts with airlines all around the world. In fact, they bundle an incredible 92% of Trent engine sales with service contracts. By monitoring engines while the planes are still flying, they can have maintenance crews ready to go when the planes touch down. They can service the engines at a lower cost than the airlines while still earning a healthy profit.

The opportunities for optimization are endless. The city where I live recently installed garbage cans that monitor how much garbage is inside. They only get emptied when they're full, not according to some arbitrary schedule, where some are still empty while others are overflowing. The result is a more efficient and effective garbage removal system.

Any task that's completed according to an arbitrary schedule is an opportunity for optimization. Find ways to incorporate sensors, allowing for an only-when-needed servicing schedule. It's a quick way to save time and reduce employee wages.

What other data do you have access to? Who else could benefit from that data? Find ways to leverage the data available to you. Could you anonymize the data and sell it in non-competitive markets? Could you start a new business model and leverage the data yourself?

INRIX is a mobile traffic app. When analyzing traffic data, the developers realized that the data could be used to measure economic activity, particularly around shopping malls. They now sell their INRIX Global Traffic Scorecard for over 1,000 cities around the world, helping hedge fund managers and business analysts predict economic activity and quarterly earnings figures for publicly traded companies.

What data is inherent in your business but easy to overlook because it doesn't seem relevant? Two of the lessons in big data: First, there is data in nearly everything. And second, in sufficient quantities, even apparently silly or innocuous data can suddenly become incredibly insightful. It all starts by asking the right questions.

As mentioned earlier, we've seen big data implications in the distribution sector. Delivery routes are being optimized and processes streamlined. We've seen significant applications in the mining sector. Oil and gas exploration is being redefined by thousands of sensors in the ground, with algorithms building sophisticated models of underground geology. Refineries are using sensors to become more efficient, and the trend is occurring in renewables including solar and wind energy as well.

This is important because fossil fuels are a classically "mature" industry. Insiders have a saying: "We've already gotten the easy oil." Without the combination of IoT sensors (mounted directly on drill bits, among other places), new fracking technologies (extracting high-quality and previously inaccessible shale oil), and sophisticated data-driven geological modeling, the industry would simply run dry. It's these emergent tools that are allowing producers to drill with unprecedented precision and continued productivity.

Another fascinating application is in facilities management. Many commercial office buildings have literally thousands of sensors measuring temperature, pressure, humidity, and light, among other things. "Smart buildings" and building information modeling (BIM) systems are optimizing energy usage, water, HVAC, and security requirements.

The Hudson Yards residential real estate development in New York City is a truly smart neighborhood. The buildings are full of sensors monitoring everything from energy and water usage to air quality and noise levels. New York University's Center for Urban Science and Progress (CUSP) is analyzing the data, looking for new efficiencies in sustainable living. The United Arab Emirates (UAE) is building Masdar City in Abu Dhabi, another ambitious sustainable-living community, and there are many similar projects around the world.

Data is also being aggregated into the smart grid. "Smart cities" are collecting data in countless areas, allowing them to optimize resources across a broad spectrum of services. Already today, Singapore uses their Electronic

Road Pricing system to streamline traffic and citizens' smartphones to sense potholes, allowing authorities to schedule road maintenance. Other cities including London, Tokyo, Berlin, and Toronto are equally creative. We're optimizing our planet, and the IoT is an enabling technology. Sensors collect the data that makes optimization possible.

Abundance

Let me be clear. The world is getting better. We're moving towards a world of abundance. As products become increasingly digital, the technology becomes ubiquitous and the cost structure collapses. We used to buy cameras. Today, they're included in all smartphones. We used to buy GPS devices, flashlights, encyclopedias, and calculators. Today, they're all included.

Every industry is affected by this "demonetization," and the biggest driver is digitization. *Once a product or service is digitized, it goes through a predictable process where the technology gets cheaper and eventually approaches free.* Every year, more and more features are "included" in the products and services we buy. More and more features that used to cost money are now available free of charge (or for a nominal cost). But let's boil it down to the most fundamental resource of all: Energy. Yup, it's happening there too.

As mentioned earlier, solar power is following an exponential curve. The cost of photovoltaic (PV) solar panels is decreasing each year. Meanwhile, the efficiency of these panels is improving at the same time. Between the two, the cost per kilowatt hour is dropping below traditional energy sources like coal and natural gas.

Grid parity refers to the point at which an alternative energy source can be purchased at the same price as electricity from the local utility. Grid parity is different in each country because resources are more available in some regions than others. As the cost per solar kilowatt hour continues to drop, we're reaching grid parity in one market after another.

In 2014, Chile scrapped the Patagonia Dam Project (which was controversial for a number of reasons) and invested in solar power instead. China's National Energy Administration installed over thirty gigawatts of solar power in 2016. And in 2017, they scrapped plans for 104 new coal power plants. Forty-nine of them were already under construction! One by one, countries around the world are hitting that threshold where renewable energy is becoming cheaper than fossil fuels.

The significance of this cannot be overstated. When a country hits grid parity and invests in renewable energy infrastructure at scale, the increased production volume inevitably reduces the cost structure even further. That means the new technology (such as PV panels, for example) becomes even more competitive in the future, accelerating the transition. We're starting to hit that inflection point with solar power.

Government policies (like Donald Trump's push for coal and reduction of subsidies for renewable energy) will affect when we achieve grid parity here in America, but it won't stop it from happening. Meanwhile, production and refining costs for fossil fuels are fairly stable. Policies in favor of fossil fuels will only delay grid parity, not eliminate it.

Of course, there are many other sources of energy, and some of those are scaling as well. The next twenty years will bring dramatic increases in renewables, contributing to an increasingly abundant supply of clean and inexpensive energy. It's simply a matter of supply and demand. Demand for energy is growing, yes, but the supply of renewables is growing at an accelerating rate.

What happens when energy becomes abundant and inexpensive? For starters, we can desalinate water. Water covers 71% of our planet. It should be an abundant resource, but it's not. The problem, of course, is the salt. But if energy was abundant, it would make sense economically to desalinate ocean water. Also, if energy was inexpensive, we could pump that water inland to irrigate unused land.

All you need is abundant energy. I know it seems like a distant reality, but the trends clearly point in that direction. Desalination plants already operate all around the world, including huge plants in Saudi Arabia, the UAE, and Israel. If you have abundant energy, abundant water becomes possible as well. And with energy and water taken care of, the ecosystem of the entire planet changes. This "distant" reality is coming sooner than you think.

On top of that, birth rates are dropping all around the world, which means that the world population is stabilizing. According to the World Bank, we're almost guaranteed to hit eleven billion people in the next 100 years, but the populations will recede after that. Birth rates have already dropped below replacement rate in most developed countries. Within 200 years, the population will likely stabilize between seven and nine billion. With abundant energy, this planet can sustain that.

Health metrics are improving as well. Life expectancy is increasing, infant mortality is dropping, deaths by disease are dropping, even deaths by natural disaster are dropping. Most people have no idea. They actually think the broad metrics of human health and longevity are getting worse. Nothing could be further from the truth.

The problem is that our media only covers bad news. As humans, we're hardwired to notice bad news more than good news. And since the news media is in the business of delivering our eyeballs to their advertisers, bad news is simply better for business. We're constantly inundated with bad news, but the truth is quite different. The truth is actually very good, and it continues to improve.

Politicians are just as bad. People are more motivated by fear than hope. It's the same human bias of prioritizing bad news over good news, so it's common for politicians to resort to fearmongering to motivate their base. Donald Trump took this to the extreme in his 2016 campaign. Many of his supporters believe that the world is falling apart at the seams, but it's not true.

That's not to suggest that the world is perfect already. Far from it. Countless things need fixing. The problems Trump trumpeted on the campaign trail are real, but they're only part of the story. Those bad things are happening amidst an improving world. Even though there are still plenty of problems, overall, life on Earth is improving. Steven Pinker's new book, touted by

Bill Gates, titled *Enlightenment Now* discusses this in detail.

Tomorrow's leaders need an optimistic perspective in order to exploit emerging business opportunities. Opportunities are everywhere, but they're easy to miss if you're not looking for them. Look for opportunities! Believe that they're out there. Read optimistic books including *Abundance* and *Bold* by Peter Diamandis and Steven Kotler. They're both inspiring assessments of the technologies revolutionizing our world and the opportunities they create for businesses.

Machine Learning

There's a natural progression playing out. The collapsing cost structure in the data space was step #1. The explosion of sensors and data collection through the IoT and IIoT was step #2. Machine learning is step #3 and artificial intelligence is step #4. Each trend is a precursor to the next step.

The essential ingredient in machine learning is data . . . lots of data. The reason we've seen an explosion in machine learning is because there's been an explosion of data. The two go hand in hand.

IBM's early artificial intelligence (AI) initiative, Deep Blue, beat Kasparov at chess in 1997. There was a lot of talk about AI back then, but it wasn't really AI at all. It was just brute computational force applied to a limited number of possibilities. It wasn't machine learning, that's for sure. The algorithm didn't learn or improve in any way. It just calculated probabilities on a massive scale and generated recommendations accordingly.

This is an important distinction. Brute computational force is not machine learning. The whole idea behind machine learning is that the machine has to *learn*! It needs a way to incorporate past experience (successes and failures) into future calculations.

Deep Blue's victory over Kasparov was followed by a roughly ten-year "AI winter," with limited progress. During that time, exploding quantities of data were motivating different approaches in the field. Neural networks were first invented in 1958 but only got traction in the big data age. They emulated the human brain, allowing software to layer in progressively more complex tasks and then learn from the computations at each level.

Neural networks are a major part of modern machine learning, but they require massive amounts of data to succeed. That data started pouring in, and advancements in machine learning soon followed. Today, every single Fortune 500 company is looking for ways to incorporate machine learning into marketing, operations, and product and service offerings.

This whole process started with the collapsing cost structure for data processing, bandwidth, and storage. From there, it was natural to collect more data (the IoT and IIoT) and then leverage increasingly sophisticated analytics platforms, resulting, finally, in machine learning and artificial intelligence.

Any discussion about machine learning and artificial intelligence has to begin with these underlying trends. Elon Musk, founder of Tesla and SpaceX, talks about thinking in "first principles." The idea is to break everything down to the most fundamental truths, and reasoning up from there. The fundamental truth in technology is that data processing, bandwidth, and storage are scaling along an exponential curve.

Good, bad or indifferent, if you are not investing in new technology, you are going to be left behind.

Philip Green

SECTION TWO: AI
MACHINES LEARN DIFFERENTLY THAN HUMANS

Recent developments in artificial intelligence have been staggering. But before we dig into that, it's important to understand the role that technology plays in business. It's essentially a form of leverage that businesses can exploit to offer new products and services to their customers. *Technology is a form of leverage.* Tomorrow's leaders need to proactively leverage emerging technologies to stay ahead of the competition.

Technology = Leverage

In 2009, Brian Acton was looking for work. One of the places he applied for a job was Facebook, and Facebook turned him down. Brian's a gracious guy. At the time, he wrote a tweet about it:

"Facebook turned me down. It was a great opportunity to connect with some fantastic people. Looking forward to life's next adventure."

And what might that be? Well, he got together with a friend of his and started WhatsApp. They grew that company over the course of five years and ended up selling it to none other than Facebook for a cool $19 billion. Ah, the irony!

Not surprisingly, the pundits were out in full force, adding commentary on the transaction. There are a number of different ways you can look at it. First, at the time of the sale, the company had fifty-five employees, so by that measure, Facebook paid $345 million per employee. Second, at the time of the sale, the company had 450 million active monthly users, so by that measure, Facebook paid $42 per user. But regardless of the calculation, it's an awful lot of money!

Perhaps the most interesting way to look at this transaction, though, is that over just five years, a group of fifty-five employees managed to engage over 450 million active monthly users. Five years is not a long time. For me, five years ago seems like just yesterday. But in that short period of time, fifty-five people built something that engaged almost half a billion people. That demonstrates the *leverage* in the system.

This is one of the most important concepts in this book: *There is more and more leverage in the system all the time.* Although there are many forms of leverage, technology represents the primary example. Technology is a form of leverage.

We've all heard stories about the division between rich and poor, and those stories are true. The division between rich and poor is growing every year. Much of that is a function of this leverage.

There are some people and some businesses who are leveraging technology and, for the most part, they're doing really well. Meanwhile, the majority of people (and businesses too) are being leveraged by the exact same technology. And for them, it's increasingly difficult to squeeze out a living.

As business leaders, we always have to ensure that we're on the right side of the leverage equation. With technology evolving along an exponential curve, it's even more important. If you wait too long, it's impossible to catch up.

You have to run towards innovation, not run away from it. You have to embrace new technologies, not shy away from them. You have to actively challenge existing systems and look for ways to disrupt the status quo.

Any time you discuss innovation, regardless of the context, it really boils down to just one concept which can be summarized in two words: *Budgeting failure.* Innovation requires that you budget for failure. It requires that you try new things, which implies that they may not work.

Amazon founder and CEO, Jeff Bezos, is brilliant. He once said, "If you know it's gonna work, it's not an experiment." It's true. In order to be innovative, you have to try things that you don't know will work. Some will. Others won't. If you don't have a budget for those failures, innovation becomes impossible.

Jeff Bezos also said that any intelligent business person would eagerly accept a 10% chance for a 100x return. Mathematically, it's a no-brainer. Over sufficient attempts, you'll end up with a 10x return. You'll still fail 90% of the time! That's a fascinating perspective. A mathematical no-brainer results in a 90% failure rate.

In order to stay on the right side of the leverage equation, innovation is imperative. And innovation guarantees periodic failures, so create a budget for that up front. That's the only way to formally add innovation to your corporate strategy. That's the only way to stay on the right side of the leverage equation.

There are lots of examples of leverage through technology. Software is a form of leverage. You can leverage software. The cloud is a form of leverage. You can leverage the cloud. You can leverage mobile technology. You can increasingly leverage wearable technology. Dozens of cool wearable technologies are being introduced. How can you use these technologies?

Virtual and augmented reality (VR/AR) are other examples. These technologies are emerging quickly. Most people think they'll be limited to video games, but there are so many other applications! Virtual reality offers tremendous opportunities for product training and virtual conferencing. Augmented reality promises to increase productivity in technical fields, delivering specifications and instructions to workers in real time.

Even better, once a VR/AR headset achieves broad market adoption, we'll soon see an augmented Internet where companies compete with each other to create immersive

VR/AR experiences, just as they compete with their websites today. Within a few years, you'll be able to visit thousands of increasingly creative and immersive VR/AR experiences provided for free by companies striving to attract, inspire, and engage their customers.

We've already seen a number of museums using augmented reality to enhance their exhibits. Coca-Cola teamed up with Spotify to create an augmented reality social music app. Maybelline L'Oréal and Argos have both used similar technology to engage their customers. Healthcare companies are using it to explain bone diagnoses, identify veins underneath the skin, and direct surgeries remotely. All major business-to-consumer (B2C) brands will soon be scrambling to develop their own VR/AR experiences as part of their broader marketing and branding strategies.

Do you work for a B2C company? If so, do you have a strategy to leverage VR/AR technology? It'll sneak up on most businesses. If you could go back in time, knowing how big the Internet has become, how much sooner would you have adopted an online marketing strategy? Developing immersive VR/AR experiences for the augmented Internet will soon be unavoidable for consumer brands.

Does your company sell to other businesses? That's often referred to as business-to-business or B2B. If so, start looking for applications in your field. What experiences (equipment training, emergency procedures, etc.) can you deliver to your customers in a virtual environment? What information (specifications, instructions, etc.) could you deliver in an augmented environment?

Robotics is another technology to leverage. Assembly line automation continues to evolve, but the more exciting area involves robots that can work alongside human employees. The Baxter and Sawyer robots (by Rethink Robotics) are cases in point. Both are specifically designed to work alongside humans, and their capabilities are increasing every year.

Amazon is leveraging robotics. Their distribution facilities are enormous and contain thousands of shelving units. The employees don't need to walk up and down long aisles to access these shelving units. Instead, small transport robots pick up the product-laden shelving units and navigate them directly to the front of the facility. Once the items are picked and packed, the shelving units are brought back to their assigned location in the warehouse.

Other warehousing operations are using drones to verify inventory. These tedious jobs were historically filled by human workers, and the output was notoriously prone to human error. Drones can do the same job in the middle of the night (with the lights turned off) without fatigue, boredom, or lunch breaks.

The Tesla factory is located just a few miles down the road from my home. The facility is almost entirely automated. An automobile manufacturing plant would never be possible in California if it weren't for robotics. California isn't exactly a factory-friendly place. Real estate is expensive, labor costs are high, and there are lots of regulations. But automation in their plant requires far fewer employees than historical equivalents. Tesla is leveraging robotics.

In recent years, we've seen the introduction of concierge and security robots at airports, shopping malls, convention centers and hotels. Airports are particularly interesting to follow. Flight check-in, food ordering, and customs screening are all being replaced with automated touch-screen kiosks. It will soon be happening everywhere.

The satellite industry is making waves as well. Most people immediately think about rocket technology, and that is certainly evolving quickly. But the other big innovation in satellites is their size. The smartphone in your pocket has more processing power and memory than 90% of the satellites orbiting our planet. Companies are building satellites about the size of coffee mugs and launching entire constellations of satellites rather than one big one, reducing the cost by orders of magnitude.

These are all forms of leverage. Think about your business. Think about ways you could incorporate these technologies in your production and/or delivery process.

One of my favorite quotes is by William Gibson: "The future is already here—it's just not evenly distributed." You don't have to reinvent the wheel. Just keep your eye on the cutting edge. Watch for new use cases and success stories. Follow the venture capital and private equity money. Follow POCs and pilot programs. And along the way, ask yourself how you can incorporate the same technologies in your own business.

Institutional Blindness

Patrick Dixon, author of *The Future of Almost Everything*, talks about "institutional blindness." After working at a corporation or within a given industry for as little as three weeks, you already start to have tunnel vision. You develop blind spots. It's natural. You have deadlines, project milestones, and quarterly earnings calls to prepare for. You're busy! And whenever you focus on one task, you invariably miss other developments taking place outside your field of vision.

Daniel Simons and Christopher Chabris conducted a now-famous selective attention test in 1999. It involved students wearing either black or white t-shirts, passing basketballs to each other. When asked to count the number of passes the white students completed, most viewers focused on the task and completely missed a person wearing a gorilla costume walking through the group in the middle of the timed exercise.

I remember watching this video for the first time. I knew it was a test and concentrated on my assigned task as instructed, and I too missed the gorilla. After watching the video again, I was stunned that I had missed it the first time around. It was such a striking demonstration of selective attention. The gorilla even did a little dance while in the middle of the group. I missed it entirely.

This is exactly how institutional blindness works. We focus on certain activities and specific deadlines, making it inevitable that we miss often-obvious developments that might threaten the very business we're trying to perfect. This happens all the time with technology, and its exponential nature makes it even more dramatic.

That's the value of having an outside speaker at your events, by the way. It jolts people out of their silos and nudges their subconscious minds to notice new things. I can't imagine the things I probably miss each day as a result of selective attention. It's horrifying, actually. The worst part is that I have no idea what I'm missing!

The most important objective at events should be to generate buzz and get people talking to each other. That's what generates new ideas. And to get that process started, find someone to share inspiring case histories and success stories with the group. This will leave your attendees thinking more expansively and open them up to new ways of doing things.

We'll be covering a broad range of technologies in this book. Stop yourself along the way and ask how you can leverage these technologies yourself. Consider the implications of each one and let your mind wander beyond the confines of your specialty or your industry. Pretend you're looking down from 40,000 feet. Pretend you're the puppet master, in charge of the whole thing. What would you do? How would you capitalize on these trends?

Artificial Intelligence

Artificial intelligence is exciting to follow because new milestones are being achieved at an accelerating rate. Many AI success stories are already well known, but it's instructive to review the accelerating pace of developments. For example, IBM's Deep Blue beat Kasparov at chess in 1997. It took fourteen years before another similar milestone was reached, when IBM's Watson won at *Jeopardy* in 2011.

Later that same year, Apple introduced Siri. That's a very different type of AI, but it definitely qualifies in the category. Google introduced their Google Now in the following year, and Microsoft caught up two years later

(April, 2014) with Cortana. Amazon's Alexa was released in November of that same year.

Tesla introduced their autopilot mode, another exploding field of artificial intelligence, in October 2015. The autonomous Olli bus started operating in a designated London neighborhood in June 2016, and the nuTonomy autonomous taxi service launched in Singapore two months later. Uber started autonomous driving pilots in America the following month.

The autonomous Google car is expected to launch in 2018, GM has promised a fully autonomous vehicle by 2019, and Ford has promised one by 2021: No steering wheel, no pedals! Volkswagen recently unveiled their Sedric concept car, and there are plenty of other concepts hitting the markets as well.

Zoox is a particularly appealing example. They've raised over $200 million so far. The car looks like a futuristic racecar from the *Blade Runner* movie, configured exactly the same way whether it's driving forward or backward. If it's autonomously driven, it really doesn't matter if it's going forward or backward. The passengers sit on either side, facing each other.

Autonomous Vehicles

What happens when autonomous vehicles gain traction in consumer markets? They're coming way faster than people think! We're already seeing the impact of the inexpensive Uber service. People in city centers aren't buying cars as much. They're using Uber instead. The overall cost is lower and they no longer have to look (or pay) for parking. In his book *The High Cost of Free*

Parking, Donald Shoup suggested that 30% of cars in congested urban settings are, in fact, just looking for parking!

With autonomous vehicles, car sales will fall further. It will start in city centers and fan out from there. People won't buy cars. Instead, they'll have a subscription for an autonomous car service: perhaps 1,000 or 1,500 miles per month. They'll just order a car on their smartphone, catch the ride, and then get out at their destination, allowing the car to pick up someone else and keep driving.

Vehicles have one of the lowest utilization rates of any large-scale individual purchase. The average utilization rate is just 6%. That means the average car is parked 94% of the time. With autonomous vehicles, the average utilization rate changes completely, especially in congested city centers. Autonomously driven car services will approach 100% utilization while demand for parking structures will almost disappear.

There are some people who anticipate a 90% reduction in automobile sales in the coming twenty years. I think that's high, but the logic is sound. What happens if automobile sales drop by 60% or even 40%? It's a huge industry. The Alliance of Automobile Manufacturers states that the automobile sector (suppliers, manufacturers, and dealers) employs 7.25 million Americans. That's about 3.8% of the US workforce. Imagine the impact on the economy if sales dropped significantly.

For context, US car sales dropped about 30% between 2006 and 2009 during the financial crisis and great recession, and that was enough to require government bailouts for manufacturers to survive. If we have another sales shock of that magnitude or bigger, especially if it's part of a long-term structural trend, we can expect a major impact on our employment markets.

Otto ran a POC with its autonomous truck in 2016. The truck drove 125 miles down a Colorado freeway towards Colorado Springs, autonomously driven. There was a guy in the cab, but he wasn't driving. The payload was 50,000 cans of Budweiser. Everything arrived just fine.

Imagine the implications. There are 1.7 million truck drivers in the United States, and a total of 3.5 million people who operate commercial vehicles for a living. What happens to those jobs?

To be clear, the Otto truck didn't drive all the way to the final destination in Colorado Springs. Instead, it drove to a transport hub outside the city. From there, the driver took control and drove it the last two or three miles. Another option is to operate the truck as a drone for the last few inner-city miles, with the "driver" sitting in a cubicle using all the standard controls (including a steering wheel, brakes, accelerator, and live video footage from the actual vehicle) to navigate the truck to its final destination.

So the trucking jobs won't disappear entirely, but the long-haul will soon be done autonomously and the inner-city miles might be controlled from a remote office building somewhere. Unfortunately, for the drivers, the money is in the long-haul. That's where they earn good money. When this technology gains traction, the long-haul disappears, and they'll lose the majority of their earning potential.

For the exact same reason, transport companies have a big incentive to implement this technology. The savings are massive. And once one trucking company deploys the technology, they'll gain a significant competitive advantage, forcing all the others to follow suit. Once this begins, industry-wide adoption will happen quickly.

Tesla unveiled their new 100% electric Tesla Semi in late 2017. According to the CEO and founder, Elon Musk, these trucks are 20% cheaper than traditional diesel trucks on a per mile basis, and their range is 500 miles on a single charge. Tesla Semis come standard with the hardware for autonomous driving. Companies including Walmart, Pepsi, UPS, and Anheuser-Busch were quick to place preorders.

The incredible thing is that we currently have a shortage of truck drivers in the United States, and it's expected to get worse. There are bidding wars to find drivers. So in the short run, we have a shortage. In the long run, we'll have a surplus. This industry will inevitably undergo a dramatic U-turn within the next five or ten years.

The bottleneck is regulation. The technology is already in place, and the hardware (the actual trucks) will be on the road soon. Once regulations are in place, the trucking industry will be disrupted. Commercial drivers represent about 1% of the US population and about 2% of its workforce. This one innovation could increase the US unemployment rate by two percentage points.

Highway driving is very different than city driving. The technology for highway driving already exists, and regulations will soon follow. The technology for city driving, on the other hand, is still a work-in-progress. City autonomous driving needs to recognize and distinguish between thousands of possible scenarios.

Imagine a truck with a stop sign painted on the side. Humans would immediately recognize that it's not a road signal. How could an algorithm make that same distinction? Imagine a person using hand signals to direct traffic manually. Humans would understand that easily. Not so for algorithms. These endless permutations will get figured out eventually, but there's still work to do.

There are about 250,000 taxi drivers in America. How many Uber and Lyft drivers are there? All of these drivers are on the wrong side of the leverage equation. They will soon be displaced by autonomous driving technology, and it's not easy to retrain people from one industry for another. These technologies will generate profits for large corporations, but they'll inevitably displace workers at the same time.

Yet again, we see both the positive and negative effects of technology. Both perspectives are valid. Autonomous driving will deliver operational efficiencies while reducing accidents. It will also push more people into the fend-for-yourself category. It will push more people into the gig economy of freelance work and side hustles. It will push more people towards anarchy.

How long will it take for autonomous vehicles to dominate our roadways? The entire fleet of vehicles in the US (about 250 million cars and trucks) has an average age of about eleven years (according to IHS Automotive). Even if every new car was capable of autonomous driving, it would still take at least eleven years for the fleet to be fully replaced.

Of course, there's an adoption curve that will play out as well. The transition will happen first in urban centers and will take much longer in rural communities. Some car enthusiasts will continue driving long after autonomous vehicles become the norm, but many will switch quickly. If car sales drop dramatically at the same time, urban roads could be dominated by autonomous vehicles within twenty years.

What happens between now and then? Imagine a world where one third of cars are autonomously driven. Human drivers will start interacting with these drone cars on the road, causing a whole new set of problems. People will soon learn how autonomous vehicles react in different situations. Young drivers will treat them like obstacles in an augmented reality video game, perhaps even scoring points along the way. Videos will be uploaded, showing driving interactions with drone cars, encouraging increasingly unsafe maneuvers.

Laws will be enacted, prohibiting human drivers from intentionally manipulating drone cars. Eventually, automobile accidents will be caused almost entirely by human drivers. Authorities will propose restrictions on human driving, but those proposals will fall on deaf ears. It will take time, and a host of crazy situations, for societies to find a functional balance between human drivers and drone cars.

Many technologists describe utopian futures without acknowledging the transition period between now and then. These transitions will take time. They will bring chaotic situations and regulatory missteps. The transitions will cause most of the problems, as people and regulators adapt to new realities. One thing is for sure: It will be a wild ride!

Fleet Learning

When Tesla first introduced their autopilot function, a number of Tesla owners started posting videos on YouTube, reporting their cars learning and improving from their daily driving patterns. One owner reported the car mistakenly taking left-turn lanes along the freeway. After a few days of correcting the car manually, it learned to avoid these left-hand turn lanes without manual assistance. Another owner reported his car learning to slow down for the 113N exit ramp from California 80E towards Sacramento.

The important thing to understand is that these improvements weren't limited to the individual cars involved. Every single Tesla benefited from them at the same time! They call it "fleet learning" and it's a core characteristic of modern cloud-computing-based platforms.

Every individual Tesla owner experiences different situations as they drive their cars. All of this data is transmitted up to the cloud where the central technology platform resides. Every new experience, by any individual driver, improves the capabilities of the entire fleet.

The data (combined with cloud computing) is facilitating the process. Tesla is accumulating vast amounts of real-life driving data. They're learning and improving and fixing problems along the way.

There was a Tesla fatality in 2016. It happened because a semi-truck turned left across a Florida freeway and an oncoming Tesla Model S drove right underneath it at 74 MPH, tearing off the roof and killing the driver instantly. The problem was that the truck's white trailer blended in with the white overcast skies. The Tesla literally didn't see it. The brakes were never activated. But as horrific as the accident was, it allowed Tesla to learn and improve. They reduced the reliance on the camera data and increased the reliance on sonar, fixing the problem.

Over the years ahead, there will be plenty of accidents in unique situations, and some may have horrible outcomes. But in each case, the car company will investigate the situation and fix the problems. The situation in Florida will never happen again, at least not in the same way. That particular problem is fixed. Each accident will inevitably result in improvements.

Imagine if every aspect of your life operated this way. Each time a mistake is made, the models improve to eliminate that particular mistake in the future. Now, imagine any mistake that *anybody* makes having the same result for everyone connected to the network. Each person would benefit from the experiences of the entire group. That's fleet learning. That's the future.

AlphaGo, a machine learning platform designed to play the game of Go, is another interesting case history. Go is a board game popular in Asian countries. It's somewhat similar to chess but is exponentially more complex. When Deep Blue won at chess in 1997, it was a function of brute-force computational power. There is no way to apply the same approach to Go. There are simply too many possible options.

DeepMind is the company that developed the AlphaGo platform. The company is based in the UK and was purchased by Google in 2014. They took a machine learning approach to the challenge. First, they gave the platform 100,000 human games: games from competitions where every move had been recorded. The platform had one simple objective: Mimic human behavior. Use the initial data to anticipate what a human would do in each situation.

Once the platform processed the data, they instructed it to play itself thirty million times—more games than any human could play in an entire lifetime, or even ten lifetimes. During this second phase, they gave the platform a new objective: Avoid past errors. The AlphaGo platform then crunched through thirty million Go games, improving incrementally from each one.

With those two simple steps, AlphaGo was able to beat the world champion, Lee Sedol, in South Korea in March 2016. AlphaGo won four out of five games, a decisive victory. Most experts didn't think this would be possible for at least ten more years!

The most interesting part of this story occurred after the tournament was over. The developers from DeepMind reviewed the computer logs to see how the platform selected its moves. There was one move in particular that flummoxed players and commentators alike. It was move #37 in the second game. The probability of a human making that move was roughly one in 10,000, yet AlphaGo used its own experience to make the selection. The developers were unable to follow the process it used. It was literally an inhuman move.

It's definitely interesting to see how machine learning platforms accumulate knowledge. They learn differently than humans. A group of Australian researchers instructed a machine learning platform to use lasers to manipulate and minimize particle movement in a low-density gas. By minimizing particle movement, they're essentially removing heat, making the particles colder.

In 2001, Eric Cornell and Carl Wieman won the Nobel Prize in Physics for successfully creating the Bose-Einstein condensate, a state of matter theorized by Satyendra Nath Bose and Albert Einstein in 1924. The state is so cold—even colder than outer space—that microscopic quantum phenomena can be detected. Cornell and Wieman studied this theoretical state for decades and finally created it in a lab environment in 1995.

The Australian machine learning platform re-created the Bose-Einstein condensate in less than one single hour! When the researchers reviewed the computer logs, they were astonished at what they found. The platform had used strategies that the Nobel laureates had never even considered. The platform had approached the problem in a completely different way. But in the end, it produced the same end result in a fraction of the time.

It's difficult to build machine learning platforms that operate the way you intend at the beginning. But once you succeed, it's amazing how powerful they can be. These platforms learn quickly, along an exponential curve, and evaluate data very differently than you and me. How can you incorporate machine learning into your business? What mysteries could it unlock for you?

The *MIT Technology Review* published an article in January 2017, entitled "AI Software Learns to Make AI Software." Google's AutoML platform learned to do the same thing, using deep reinforcement learning to produce a best-in-class image recognition system without human assistance. Progress is accelerating! The fastest supercomputer in the world is the Tianhe-2 in Guangzhou, China, running 3.1 million Intel cores! The Sunway TaihuLight, also in China, has over 10 million cores. China is investing heavily in these technologies.

The 2nd Wave

Stories about exponential machine learning fuel speculation that artificial intelligence will eventually dominate humans and take over the world. Respected thought leaders including Elon Musk, Stephen Hawking, and Bill Gates have all warned about the dangers of AI. There's definitely a risk, particularly of a single monolithic AI, but that type of general intelligence remains years in the future and will be balanced by other integrated platforms. I don't anticipate a war with machines any time soon. The bigger risk might be the malicious application of AI technologies by rogue actors.

New technologies follow a predictable pattern of adoption. The first wave of users includes academic researchers, government, and business. For the most part, they play by the rules. Later, when the technology becomes ubiquitous and inexpensive, a second wave of users emerges. This second wave is much more diverse and creative. They start using the same technology in a wide variety of situations and, in some cases, for nefarious purposes.

Think about social media. The first wave included corporations using social media to market their products and services. Millions of artists, musicians, authors, politicians, and industry experts used social media to accumulate followers online. But a few years later, the so-called Islamic State (also known as ISIL or ISIS) started using social media to spread their message of hate and Islamic Jihad. The hacking group Anonymous uses social media to attract new members and coordinate attacks. ISIS and Anonymous are part of the second wave.

Additive manufacturing (3D printing) is going through a similar progression. The first wave included applications in prototyping, medical advancements, and equipment maintenance on the International Space Station, all exciting and admirable innovations. As 3D printers have come down in price, however, we now see designs posted online to print gun parts and other restricted items. That's the second wave.

The same is true for big data. The first wave included people from business and government. Obviously, you could argue that these early applications involved manipulative, profit-maximizing or surveillance-based objectives, but they still fell mostly within expected channels. But as time passes and the power of big data analytics becomes ubiquitous, it's being used by hackers and criminals for clearly illegal purposes. They are part of the second wave.

This pattern will unfold with AI as well. The first wave includes academic researchers and big corporations, and the applications are following established expectations. But in time, it will become accessible for rogue players who will use it for destructive purposes. Imagine a brilliant fifteen-year-old hacker in Kazakhstan who builds an AI whose sole purpose is to cause chaos. That's guaranteed to happen sooner or later.

It will be important to put safeguards in place to prevent these types of situations. Elon Musk and Peter Thiel, among others, have helped to create OpenAI, a non-profit organization devoted to discovering and enacting the path to safe artificial general intelligence.

What's the new technology in your industry? Who could use that technology for nefarious purposes? If it cost just 1% of the current price, who would use it to cause chaos or hurt others? Think exponentially. These patterns are predictable.

In late 2016, Jonathan Kolber wrote a fascinating article for the *Institute for Ethics and Emerging Technologies*. Once computers evolve to be exponentially more powerful than humans, he argued, we'll be about as interesting to AI as growing trees are to us. We'll just operate far too slowly. We'll become irrelevant. In this scenario, AI would only engage with humans if we somehow threatened its essential inputs; namely energy and the necessary computing infrastructure. As long as the AI has what it needs, it may choose to ignore us entirely.

These hypothetical scenarios are just that: hypothetical. I mention them here because there are opinions on both sides. Some experts are optimistic, others are apocalyptic, but there are plenty of smart people monitoring developments, and I place my trust in them. For now, let's focus on the opportunities of AI, not the catastrophic humanity-ending scenarios.

Business Opportunities

Think back to the 1960s, 70s, and 80s. Electricity was being added to everything. Electric toothbrushes and lawnmowers were introduced. Electric kitchen mixers and screwdrivers became common. One product category after another was evaluated to see if it could be improved with electricity. Even candles have now been replaced by look-alike electric alternatives. They were all business opportunities, and savvy entrepreneurs and executives took advantage.

Now, think about the upcoming 2020s and 30s. What will the growing technology be then? I guarantee that AI will factor high on that list, and savvy businesses will be adding AI to everything. This evolution will follow the exact same process as electricity did, so think about the products and services in your industry. Which ones could benefit from AI? It's only a matter of time. Someone will make that happen. Why can't it be you?

AI already surrounds us. Our email spam folders use AI to identify junk mail. Netflix and Pandora use AI to generate personalized recommendations. Smartphones all have AI interfaces such as Siri and Google Now. Amazon Alexa and Google Home are bringing AI into our own homes, and this is just the beginning.

Companies are working to incorporate AI into toilets along with sensors to scan and evaluate urine and stools for health metrics. Amazon's new Echo Look can tell you which outfits look the most flattering on your body and will soon be able to give advice on everything from haircuts to complementary color palettes. Airports are using facial recognition to process security checks as soon as you arrive, and police departments are using machine learning to anticipate crimes before they happen.

This transition is happening whether you profit from it or not. We're heading towards a world of intelligent everything. AI will be incorporated into everything, and each application represents another business opportunity. Stay on the right side of the leverage equation. Find ways to incorporate these technologies in your own business.

Stock Market Trading

One clear application of machine learning is in the stock market. If AlphaGo can play itself thirty million times, getting better each time, machine learning can certainly use real-time stock market data to learn predictable trading patterns. It would be no different from playing video games such as Space Invaders or Breakout, both of which were mastered by AlphaGo in a day or two.

Such platforms already exist, no doubt. Money managers around the world are shoveling stock market trading data into machine learning platforms to see if they can learn to trade profitably. If I had direct access to machine learning developers, I'd do the exact same thing! Of course, anyone who develops a platform like that would want to keep it secret, allowing them to rack up profits without encouraging competition, thereby affecting the very trading patterns being exploited.

Google launched their open source TensorFlow platform in 2015. It leverages neural network architecture to process and learn from large datasets. As an open source platform, anyone can develop applications on top of it, and I'm quite sure many people have tried to use TensorFlow for stock market, futures, FOREX, and options-trading purposes.

The beauty for Google is that they gain visibility into all of these experiments. They're receiving all the data and benefiting as a result. That's the tradeoff. They provide

and support the technology platform free of
but they also harvest the data along the way. The
to see what's working and what isn't. That's extrem
valuable data!

There's an important distinction between AI-based stock
market trading and traditional algorithmic trading. The
AI version implies that machine learning is improving
the platform over time. Traditional algorithmic trading uses back-testing data, variable optimization, and
walk-forward analysis to develop quantitative trading
systems. These systems do not learn with new data. On
the contrary, they have to be manually re-optimized on
a regular basis to incorporate the latest trading data into
the back-testing.

In the interest of full disclosure, I have a significant
portion of my own investment capital in an algorithmic
trading program. It's a combination of seven algorithms
that trade concurrently in the market for futures contracts. Some are designed to profit in bull markets, some
in bear markets, and some when the market is going
sideways. The objective is to deliver consistent returns
that are uncorrelated to stock market performance.

I'm regularly asked about my experience with algorithmic
trading. If you're curious about that as well, I've posted
some additional details here:

https://www.patrickschwerdtfeger.com/algorithms/

AI is guaranteed to make a splash in investment circles.
It's only a matter of time before machine learning invest-
ment vehicles become available to individual investors.
The AIEQ ticker symbol was launched in 2017. It's an

nd (ETF) that uses quantitative mod-
atson to identify and invest in specific
d estate investment trusts.

f, anyone can invest in this technology, and I
cee many more dynamic ETFs (also called "active"
s) will be introduced in the years to come. I have
oney invested in AIEQ as well and follow developments
closely. Keep an eye on this trend and evaluate new
investment options as they become available. Intelligent
and "learning" investment vehicles will definitely play a
role in future wealth management strategies.

Data-Driven Management

Artificial intelligence is making its way into management circles as well. This began with big data analytics
and is evolving from there. Software platforms (ERP,
CRM, etc.) are providing benchmarking data and operational insights through sophisticated data-visualization
dashboards. Over time, competitive providers will try
to outdo each other with increasing capabilities and
intuitive user interfaces.

Microsoft Power BI is an analytics platform specifically
designed for people without technical or programming
expertise. The platform allows users to combine private
and public datasets and obtain sophisticated insights
within minutes. Data.gov already has over 200,000 datasets publicly available (with about 10,000 datasets being
added each month), fueling an entire cottage industry
of data-driven consultants and business advisors.

The delineation between analytics and AI is murky. What
constitutes artificial intelligence versus simply good

analytics? Regardless of the delineation you use, businesses are becoming increasingly data-driven. Industry leaders might develop their own custom technology, but most of these analytics capabilities will propagate through ERP platforms. How can you stay ahead of the curve?

I've worked with a number of ERP providers over the years, and they all say the same thing. The vast majority of their customers only use a tiny percentage of their platform's capabilities. Their developers are coding increasingly powerful capabilities, yielding actionable insights, but they're almost never used. Sound familiar? We discussed the same dynamic with respect to performance insights gleaned from IoT sensors.

Consider Microsoft Excel. Everybody uses it, but most only use a small fraction of its full capabilities. The program has dozens of advanced features including visual basic for applications (VBA), vlookup, offsets, pivot tables, macros, and simulations. Very few people are comfortable with these functions, but they're all powerful in their own right. The easiest way to increase data-driven efficiencies is to better utilize the ERP platform you're already paying for.

Train your people! Allocate time on a regular basis to dig deep into the software platforms you're using. Call the provider (Oracle, SAP, Epicor, etc.) and ask them to send someone out to conduct training sessions. In most cases, that type of support is included in the price you paid. This is the lowest-hanging fruit in the strategic use of data within your organization.

It won't take long and you'll have some individuals who develop true expertise on the platform. A friend of mine has recently become obsessed with his company's SAP platform. He loves it. It appeals to his process orientation and he's discovering new possibilities all the time. When I spoke with him last, he described a report he generated which ended up on the CEO's desk. He was thrilled, and so was the CEO.

There's a big difference between familiarity and knowledge. When it comes to ERP platforms, most people only know the capabilities they need for their specific jobs. They have familiarity, but nothing more. Meanwhile, the platform is capable of delivering powerful insights and transforming the way you run your business. That requires knowledge.

There's enormous power in the software you already have. Commit to fully utilizing its capabilities. It'll take time to train everyone, but the payoffs will soon follow.

Socialbots

One of the areas advancing quickly right now is socialbot technology; the ability of having functional conversations with machines. Siri, Google Now, and Amazon's Alexa are all built on socialbot technology. These platforms are still a bit clunky, but they're improving rapidly. In a few short years, they'll be able to interact in a natural way most of the time.

The challenge is to contextualize consecutive questions. I can say "Alexa, what's the temperature outside?" and get an answer. But if I want to ask a supplemental question relating to the first, it doesn't work. I have to say "Alexa" again and ask the second question from scratch. It won't take long before these platforms can connect one question (or comment) to the next, adding context along the way.

The "Turing test" was developed by Alan Turing in 1950. It evaluates a computer's ability to communicate in a way that is indistinguishable from a human. That's the milestone we're chasing. If you can't tell the difference between a machine and a human, the use cases explode.

This technology is already being implemented in customer service departments. When you call a customer service call center, you're often invited to ask simple questions to the automated system. We've all heard, "You can say 'account balance,' 'recent transactions,' or 'make a payment.'" Perhaps the system can handle 10% or 20% of questions autonomously. In five years, that percentage will grow, perhaps to 50% or 75%, with only a minority of calls requiring human intervention.

The big tech infrastructure companies are in a race. Every business will eventually use this technology to interact with their customers. Who will provide the functionality? That depends on who has the most natural-sounding interface.

As with any machine learning platform, the most important ingredient is data. Apple accumulates data from Siri. Google receives similar data from Google Now. Amazon gets it from their Alexa install base. What about Facebook? They didn't want to be left behind, so what did they do? They introduced an API for companies— any companies—to use their chatbot technology within the Facebook Messenger interface. This will soon include natural language processing (NLP) capabilities as well.

This was a brilliant move. All established businesses will soon feel the pressure to offer spoken-language interfaces to their customers. Facebook is offering them a way to do it for free. Why? Because it gives them data. It gives them a way to improve over time. Machine learning requires data, and Facebook knows that "conversational commerce" will play a major role in future business interactions.

Companies have a huge incentive to implement this technology. Imagine the tens of thousands of employees in India, the Philippines, and right here in America, answering customer service calls all day long. Imagine the inconsistencies in their answers and the challenge of training them to follow policies and protocols. These automated systems will dramatically reduce costs while increasing consistency at the same time.

When spoken-language interfaces improve, it's only natural that they'll handle increasingly complex tasks. It'll be easy to weave sales messages into customer service responses. Marketers can split-test countless approaches and optimize conversion metrics from these calls. It's inevitable that this technology will encroach on sales functions as well.

Alibaba, China's largest ecommerce company, recently developed an AI that performs better than humans on reading-comprehension tests. As described in the *South China Morning Post* (January 15, 2018), the neural network scored 82.44 on the Stanford Question Answering Dataset, a large-scale comprehension test that includes over 100,000 questions. Humans scored 82.304. Whether customer inquiries come in written form or spoken language, computers will be able to handle their requests.

Where will these workers go? The 2016 election of Donald Trump showcased a segment of the US population that's frustrated with the current economic system: people who feel left behind. Despite a roaring stock market and record corporate profits, their world is looking bleak. They're on the wrong side of the leverage equation. Unfortunately for them, we're just getting started. Those job losses are only just beginning. We'll have millions more in short order.

Technology is a useful servant but a dangerous master.
Christian Lous Lange

SECTION THREE: JOBS
TECHNOLOGY WILL DIMINISH THE VALUE OF HUMAN CAPITAL

A recent study by The Hackett Group revealed that the number of finance employees per billion dollars in revenue has already dropped by 40% between 2004 and 2014. Job losses are not confined to some distant future. They're already here, and it will only accelerate in the years ahead.

Job Displacement Model

Shelton Leigh "Shelly" Palmer introduced an insightful model to anticipate which job tasks are most likely to be displaced by technology. The economy basically has two types of jobs: manual and cognitive. In each category, there are repetitive tasks and non-repetitive tasks. Over time, the manual repetitive tasks will be replaced by robots. The cognitive repetitive tasks will be replaced by algorithms. The remaining non-repetitive tasks will require agile humans for the manual jobs and creative humans for the cognitive jobs.

JOBS	MANUAL	COGNITIVE
repetitive	robotics	algorithms
non-repetitive	agile humans	creative humans

Think about your company. Think about the tasks carried out by your team, or even by yourself. Which tasks are repetitive? Which are non-repetitive? Make a list and sort them by complexity. Technology is essentially climbing a ladder of complexity. It's automating increasingly complex tasks over time. That's what artificial intelligence is! We're starting to automate some very complex tasks.

Going through this process helps you plan for the future. It's a lot easier to find something when you know what you're looking for. Using this exercise, you'll have a list of tasks that are likely to be replaced, and you'll even know in what order it's likely to happen. How can you plan for that eventuality?

Back in 2013, Oxford University released a study estimating that 47% of American jobs will be replaced by automation in the coming twenty years. Combining this with Shelly's model, it would seem that repetitive tasks account for 47% of American jobs, with 53% involving non-repetitive tasks. The percentage of displaced jobs was even higher in developing countries such as China (77%) and India (69%).

The jobs most at risk include professional services (loan officers, accountants, lawyers, real estate agents, insurance brokers, taxi/truck drivers, etc.) and administrative jobs (clerks, receptionists, bookkeepers, paralegals, retail salespeople, etc.).

Consider doctors and nurses. People instinctively assume that doctors are safe and nurses are at risk. Being a doctor is such a prestigious job! But the truth is quite different. The vast majority of doctor appointments involve a limited number of diagnoses. It's a repetitive job. Meanwhile, doctors earn far more than nurses. Doctors are actually more at risk than nurses.

Doctors are paid well because they go to school for years, learning an enormous amount of information, and then using that expertise to evaluate symptoms and recommend treatment options. But the application of this expertise is simple and repetitive. Computers can do the same thing quicker, better, and cheaper than human doctors.

Nurses are very different. They need compassion and empathy. They need intuition and emotional intelligence. Their job is all about human interaction and building trust with patients. Those skills are inherently human. Many nursing tasks can be automated, but many cannot.

A useful model to anticipate doctors' roles in the future, believe it or not, is Turbo Tax. Turbo Tax asks a series of questions that guide the user through the tax preparation process. Of course, each user only sees the questions they are asked individually, but the decision tree is actually quite extensive, funneling them into a wide variety of taxation circumstances. The trick is to ask the right questions in the right order, and to ask as few questions as possible overall.

This approach will increasingly be used in medical clinics. Patients will be guided through a strategic and intuitive interface that categorizes their visit quickly and easily. Many of the diagnoses will be handled without any doctors required. Nurses and nurse practitioners, all earning less than doctors, will interact with patients where necessary. Only a small number of unusual cases will be referred to an actual doctor.

Teledoc is bringing this new model to life already. With a monthly membership and a per-consult fee, you can talk to licensed doctors within ten minutes. Companies like this are optimizing service options and redefining the medical industry along the way. Walmart, CVS, and Walgreens are all introducing healthcare clinics to provide services in a more affordable and à la carte format.

The results of all this automation will include increased efficiency for companies and lower costs for customers, both good things, but they will also include massive job losses. *People rarely understand that higher productivity (a good thing) results in higher unemployment (a bad thing).* By definition, higher productivity means it takes fewer humans to produce the same output. That's the impact of automation. It's making people more productive, thereby requiring fewer of them in the future.

The result is that the value of most human capital will drop in the years ahead. People with true leadership qualities—creativity, compassion, agility, and communication skills—will be paid well. Everyone else will compete for table scraps, further widening the division between rich and poor.

This inevitably evolves towards anarchy. Some people will earn $300,000 per year while most struggle to make minimum wage. This fuels social tensions and builds animosity between low-wage workers and highly-paid specialists. It will lead to social unrest. We'll talk more about this in Section Five.

Universal Basic Income

There's been a lot of talk recently about universal basic income. The idea is that technology will displace so many jobs that the economy could collapse as a result. There would be so many unemployed people that consumer demand would crash and corporate profits would evaporate. To balance the impact, the government would pay an unconditional basic income to all citizens, independent of any other income earned.

Proponents argue that a basic income would reduce poverty and unleash creativity within our populations. They further argue that it might be our only hope to survive the mounting job losses across the economy. The problem, of course, is that programs like this cost an enormous amount of money, and the money has to come from somewhere. Taxes would have to be raised dramatically on corporations and/or those still working. Bill Gates even proposed taxing robots.

Universal basic income may look attractive in a classroom setting but would fail in the real world. Despite platitudes proclaimed by nationalistic politicians, global trade continues to increase. Competitive pressures don't just exist within individual industries. They also exist between countries.

Universal basic income might work for five or ten years but eventually, the enormous cost and associated taxation structure would make the country less competitive in global markets. That would result in higher unemployment which, through the democratic process, would result in new governments with new policies. Eventually, the program would fail.

Universal basic income would only be possible if all countries introduced similar programs at roughly the same time, but that would never happen. Conservative countries would never attempt it because the alternative (current) approach still functions. It's far from ideal, but it functions. And if some countries had universal basic income while others did not, the competitive pressures of global trade would crush those programs eventually.

Universal basic income is the ultimate social safety net. It redistributes enormous wealth from income earners to the entire population. Taxing income earners to pay everyone a basic stipend would reduce the division between rich and poor. By paying higher taxes, the rich would have less. And through the basic income, the poor would have more. The opposite is a large and widening division between rich and poor.

Interestingly, the process of demonetization is making the lives of the poor less challenging than it used to be. One or two hundred years ago, people living at the poverty level were literally starving. They didn't have enough to eat. Today, people living at the poverty level in America (about $22,000 per year for a family of four) might have an air-conditioned home, a car, a flat-screen TV, and a smartphone or two. Technology will deliver even more in the years ahead.

To be clear, poverty is a major problem in America. I don't mean to minimize the issue. I'm only making the distinction between 19th-century poverty and 21st-century poverty. It used to cause starvation and regular street riots, especially in the summer heat. Today, it's not as bad and, as a result, less disruptive.

The point is that we may not need a universal basic income in the first place. Between demonetized products/services and the burgeoning gig economy, tomorrow's displaced workers might be able to live sustainable lives by accepting freelance gigs as needed to pay their bills. They might not be happy about it, but they probably won't starve either.

The most populous income brackets are the bottom income brackets. The poor represent a huge percent-age of the population. If they can be self-reliant and self-sufficient while living at the poverty level, they don't technically *need* to rely on government subsidies. And if they don't *need* those subsidies, they can *reject* them entirely.

Of course, many will not be self-sufficient. Many will continue to rely on government programs, but it only takes a growing minority to impact the cultural dialog. Already today, ironically, the self-reliant poor are among the most critical of those on government assistance programs.

Anarchy is a society that rejects hierarchy and power structures. Demonetization is a necessary precursor. It helps people be self-reliant and self-sufficient. The coming anarchy sits at the intersection of demonetization and decentralization, both enabled by technology. Put simply, technology leads to anarchy. We'll talk more about that in Section Five.

New Job Categories

What will the jobs of the future look like? If 47% of current jobs are wiped out in the next twenty years, what new jobs will emerge? Most of them will be jobs that we can't even imagine today. Ten years ago, who would've thought that we'd have social media managers, mobile app developers, or Uber drivers? Who would've thought we'd have independent content creators on YouTube, drone operators, or user experience designers? Countless new jobs will emerge as a result of advancing technologies, and there's no way to guess them today.

The problem is that the number of new jobs will be smaller than the jobs lost during the same time period. On top of that, displaced workers are notoriously difficult to retrain for new opportunities. It's unlikely that a displaced truck driver will retrain and become a cloud services professional later on. The new jobs will be filled by young people graduating from college. The truck drivers will have to find something else to do.

A similar process unfolded in the agricultural industry. In the 1700s, agriculture accounted for over 90% of jobs. Today, it accounts for less than 2%. Where did all those jobs go? What are they doing now? Well, that transition was easier to absorb because it took place over 200 years.

But even still, at that time, nobody would've imagined a world with contractors, nurses, and lawyers. Nobody would've imagined a world with yoga instructors, life coaches, and photographers.

According to the Department of Labor Statistics, the services sector accounts for about 80% of the American economy. Most of those jobs didn't exist in the 1700s or at a minimum, they were rare. Today, they're all common occupations in our workforce.

As productivity has gone up, requiring fewer people to actually produce the products we need, people have become increasingly creative with the services they sell to each other. Yoga instructors, massage therapists, and life coaches are good examples. It's no surprise that we're hearing more about meditation, alternative medicine, and mindfulness these days. There are more and more practitioners in those industries, so their expertise naturally filters into our cultural dialog.

We all learned about Maslow's Hierarchy of Needs in school. Once demand has been thoroughly satisfied at each level, we naturally move up the hierarchy, addressing needs for belonging, feelings of accomplishment, achieving self-actualization, and even transcendence. Many new occupations are catering to these higher-level needs.

This trend will continue in the future. As increasing numbers of people become practitioners of these holistic approaches, they will increasingly become part of our daily lives. Those who claim we're witnessing some sort of "grand awakening" on this planet are only reacting to the increasing numbers of people promoting these techniques.

Other new occupations will emerge as well. People are creative, and people *want* to work. They want to have meaning and purpose. We can only imagine the creative solutions they'll develop and sell to one another.

But new technologies don't always result in massive job losses. A great example was in the 1980s when automated teller machines (ATMs) were introduced by the banks. Everyone immediately assumed that all the tellers would soon lose their jobs, but that's not what happened at all. In fact, the total number of tellers actually continued to rise (Bureau of Labor Statistics). How was that possible?

It turns out that ATMs reduced labor costs and made it cheaper for banks to open new branches. Banks started opening branches in each neighborhood. So while the number of tellers at each branch dropped, the total number of tellers between all branches increased. These tellers were then able to perform more complex tasks, leaving the simple withdrawals and deposits to the ATMs.

Automation effectively reduces the breakeven point for opening new locations. Many grocery stores already have self-checkout lines. Amazon, Walmart, and Kroger are experimenting with stores that have no cashiers at all. If automation reduces the number of salaries needed for each location, businesses can open viable locations in less populated areas.

That model will play out in countless different service professions. There may be fewer professionals needed to perform today's level of service, but tomorrow's level of service will only be possible after the tedious, repetitive, and monotonous tasks have been automated. The professionals who remain after that transition will perform more complex tasks; tasks that are not being offered today.

Again, let's look at doctors. As basic diagnoses are handled by automated systems, doctors will focus on increasingly specialized medical needs. It will also become viable to have more doctors' offices and clinics in less densely populated areas. The trend points toward higher and higher levels of service.

It's conceivable that this could happen in the trucking industry as well. Autonomously driven trucks will be much cheaper (after eliminating the driver's salary for long hauls), possibly leading to more trucking demand overall. Human drivers will only drive urban miles (between transport hubs and final destinations) but there might be an increase in those driving jobs.

The point is that enterprising businesses will exploit profitable market opportunities based on the cost of inputs required. If costs drop (through automation), businesses will dream up new services they can offer profitably. That will lead to more extravagant services, more conveniences (such as Blue Apron, Plated, and HelloFresh "meal kit" deliveries), and more money-back guarantees.

Think about your industry. In a perfect world where all the stars align, what would your customers want? What's their absolute best-case scenario? Map it out, even if it's completely unrealistic today. What's the fantasy version of your product or service? One day, someone's going to offer that level of service. Can it be you?

Also, does your business operate storefront locations? If so, can you leverage technology to reduce the breakeven point for new locations? That would allow you to expand your footprint in the communities you serve, generating additional revenue and additional profits. Are there other areas where technology could reduce operating costs, allowing for expansions of service? Don't only focus on threats to your business. Look for opportunities to expand.

Finally, the jobs most at risk include some counterintuitive fields. Software engineers are a case in point. With technology exploding in every direction, you'd think that software engineers would be in huge demand. While that may still be true today, it won't remain true for long. Writing computer code is actually quite repetitive, and AI platforms are now learning to perform such tasks better than humans.

Software engineers will follow the same path as the bank tellers. The simple code will be produced automatically at first, allowing the software engineers to be more productive, compiling modules of code into larger and more complex systems. But over time, the threshold between simple code and complex systems will rise. Machines will do more and more of the work, requiring fewer software engineers overall.

This process will open the doors to incredibly complex and sophisticated systems; systems we can't imagine today. It will also lead to software solutions in areas that aren't currently impacted by software. Both will require software engineers in the short term, but it remains possible that software engineers become mostly unnecessary in the longer term.

There are basically three types of jobs that are safe from automation. The first category includes truly creative people, including artists, scientific researchers, and business entrepreneurs. The second category involves building complex human relationships. Nurses, teachers, and therapists all qualify. And the third involves highly unpredictable occupations. Hired guns and problem solvers come to mind, including everything from plumbers and electricians to project managers and corporate turn-around specialists.

To be clear, we're not heading towards a world with 40% unemployment. People will find things to do. The problem will be that most will earn modest incomes while a few earn a fortune. An increasing percentage of the workforce will effectively be self-employed, and that career model doesn't work for everyone. Self-employment requires motivation and discipline. Neither are particularly common.

The problem in tomorrow's job market will be the ever-increasing division between rich and poor. That will fuel frustration for regular citizens, further reduce trust in government institutions, and encourage defensive strategies for self-preservation and survival. Income inequality will push us towards anarchy. We'll discuss that more in Section Five.

Automation is going to cause unemployment, and we need to prepare for it.

Mark Cuban

SECTION FOUR: BLOCKCHAIN
BLOCKCHAIN AUTOMATES TRUST

Artificial intelligence will change the world, but it's not the only technology making waves. Blockchain protocol is equally disruptive. In fact, a lot of people believe blockchain will end up making a larger impact on the world than the Internet itself. That's a tall order, but it is indeed possible.

Blockchain Defined

Blockchain is the technology behind Bitcoin. If you've been living under a rock for the past few years, Bitcoin is a digital currency and peer-to-peer payment platform that has no central governing authority and is completely independent of national borders. Nobody controls it. Nobody can shut it down.

The backbone of Bitcoin is the blockchain. It's the enabling technology. In fact, Bitcoin was the first real-life application of blockchain protocol. Blockchain is simply a method of recording transactions, but one which is immune to hacking and manipulation. Let me explain.

Blockchain is a distributed ledger. Imagine a list of transactions. But instead of storing that list in one place, it's stored in dozens, hundreds, or even thousands of different places (called "nodes") at the same time. The network is consensus driven, so the nodes have to agree that their respective versions of the ledger are identical and accurate.

This makes the network virtually impossible to hack. Anyone attempting to hack one node would have to hack all the other nodes at the exact same time. If even one node wasn't hacked successfully at the exact right time, the inconsistency between nodes would immediately be found and corrected.

It gets even better. Every new "block" of transactions that's added to the "chain" of previous blocks (hence the name "blockchain") includes a summary of the previous block's contents. As a result, it's impossible to modify something on the blockchain because you would have to then modify every subsequent block as well.

It's worth pointing out that the Bitcoin blockchain has never been hacked. And believe me, everyone has tried! A number of exchanges and digital wallets have been hacked (including Mt. Gox, BitFloor, Poloniex, and Bitfinex), but never the Bitcoin blockchain. That's a testament to the security built into the protocol.

The net result is that blockchain technology, also called distributed ledger technology (or DLT), guarantees an accurate, unhackable, and immutable record involving parties that do not necessarily trust each other. That's extremely powerful. It means that blockchain essentially automates trust.

This is important: *Blockchain automates trust.*

Think about the implications. Every business in the world is conducting transactions with parties they don't necessarily trust. In order to protect against bad actors, they all have some form of order taking, order tracking, audit, and compliance activities. If there was an electronic ledger system that automated trust, all of those administrative functions could be reduced or eliminated.

Consider the financial sector in general. Banks and insurance companies are essentially trusted intermediaries that facilitate and record financial transactions. In theory, their entire value proposition is rendered irrelevant by blockchain technology. Blockchain replaces intermediaries. It disintermediates.

The companies most at risk from blockchain technology are banks and insurance companies. Ironically, the companies investing the most in the technology are . . . wait for it . . . banks and insurance companies! In that sense, anarchists might argue that we're running towards the abyss.

The reality is less apocalyptic. There are enormous operational efficiencies available through the use of blockchain protocol. Banks and insurance companies understand that, as does the entire Fortune 500 cohort. Any opportunity to eliminate administrative roles translates directly into profits on the bottom line.

It's true that blockchain may eventually render the entire financial sector redundant. That is one possible outcome, but it's at least ten years away. Even still, does that represent an insane long-term risk for banks and insurance companies? Of course it does. But it's also a future outcome that's largely out of their control. In the meantime, they need to leverage any and all efficiencies that are available to them.

Blockchain delivers significant efficiencies, and I'm sure every single Fortune 500 company is already doing exploratory work, conducting POCs (proofs of concept) and/or running pilot programs. And because of the way blockchain operates, widespread adoption is guaranteed. Let me explain.

In 2016, Wells Fargo and Commonwealth Bank conducted a POC that involved eighty-eight bales of cotton that were shipped from Texas to China. The transaction was detailed in a smart contract and posted on a private blockchain. This is a classic example of a transaction that would benefit from blockchain technology.

What's a smart contract? It's essentially a contract that includes if-then statements, allowing for different outcomes depending on milestones reached along the way. Imagine wills and contracts that execute themselves. In this POC, the scanning of barcodes at the customer destination automatically transferred ownership and released payment, but there could be many other milestones as well.

A transaction like this involves many players including the producer, some sort of trucking at the source, loading at the dock, customs clearance, the shipping itself, unloading at the destination port, another customs agency, a trucking company in China, and the final customer. Each of these companies have order entry, tracking, perhaps some project management, audit, and compliance activities involved, and everyone charges fees to cover those expenses.

On a private blockchain, all of these participants could maintain nodes on the network. Through the consensus process, they could all approve the terms of the transaction ahead of time. Then, with a smart contract in place that specifies the details of the transaction, it could unfold without anyone entering order details, tracking activities, or auditing details after the fact. All of the information would reside on the network for all the participants to see, rendering the audit function unnecessary.

This application of blockchain protocol delivers significant efficiencies to the supply chain management process. For any large shipping company, the efficiencies are too significant to ignore. Meanwhile, as they set up their new systems, all of the other market participants would be drawn into the mix as well. They would each have their own nodes on the network.

It's only a matter of time before a few large companies deploy blockchain technology in their supply chain management systems. Once that happens, everyone else moves over at the same time.

Imagine if a company such as Microsoft deployed blockchain across its supply chain. They probably sell to every single Fortune 500 company. If they deployed blockchain, the entire Fortune 500 cohort would be pulled into the blockchain paradigm in a single step.

s highly likely in the near future. Microsoft has
y announced their Coco Framework on their Azure
cloud platform. The Coco Framework is an enterprise
blockchain solution, so they're already developing the
infrastructure to support blockchain initiatives. It's only
logical for them to use it themselves.

The world's largest container shipping company, AP
Moller-Maersk, has already teamed up with IBM to build
an industry-wide blockchain-based trading platform. It
won't be long before this transition sweeps through the
global economy.

Keep in mind that the contents of a blockchain are
encrypted. Specific information can be run through a
"one-way hash function" before being posted on the
blockchain. A hash function converts data of an arbitrary size into data of a fixed size. A one-way hash allows
data to be converted into a hash code, but the hash
code cannot be converted back into the original data.
As such, posting hash codes on a blockchain would not
jeopardize security of the underlying data.

That would allow multiple different customers to post
their transactions to the same blockchain without reveal-
ing the specifics of their order details to each other. That's
important because it protects confidential arrangements
like preferential terms or pricing arrangements between
potentially competitive customers (or suppliers).

Even with these protections, it's likely that large companies will maintain hundreds, maybe thousands, of
separate blockchains, one for each order format, perhaps,
or one for each product category. It will simply become

a method of recording transactions in a way that red administrative functions.

Profit Potential

I live in the San Francisco Bay Area. During the 1849 California gold rush, as the saying goes, the people who profited the most were those who sold the shovels. The same will hold true for the coming blockchain revolution. The companies who profit the most will be those who facilitate the enterprise implementations of the technology. Companies such as IBM, Accenture, McKinsey, and Deloitte come to mind.

Implementing new technology at enterprise scale is no easy task. The risks are enormous. Enterprise systems can't go down. Transactions are being processed every second. It's extremely important to phase in new technologies in a controlled way. These large consulting companies specialize in that process. Their margins may be excessive, but their value is justified.

As with any new technology, the first to adopt pay the most. They're the ones who pay for the exploratory work and POCs. They're the ones who navigate through the inevitable trial and error. But if they manage to implement the technology before their competitors, they'll have exclusive rights to the incremental efficiencies and profits, at least until everyone else follows suit.

With blockchain technology, that phase will be short. Most large enterprises will end up using blockchain as a result of the early innovators who buy or sell to them. Industry by industry, blockchain-related efficiencies will replace legacy systems, reducing the overall cost structure and eventually delivering lower prices for customers. After the transition is complete, prices will be lower, but margins will probably be similar to today.

The SME (small and medium enterprise) market segment will go through the same transition. Many will be swept into the mix by larger suppliers or customers, but even the smaller and/or more independent providers will feel the pressure as efficiencies materialize across the competitive landscape. The new approach will soon propagate through the entire economy.

Just as predictive maintenance and behavioral targeting delivered the early ROI for big data initiatives, supply chain management will deliver the early ROI for blockchain. The efficiencies are clear: reduced costs, enhanced traceability, and increased trust across the network. But there are other promising applications as well, including:

- International remittances

- Digital payments

- Digital identity

- Smart assets

- Land ownership

- Clearing & settlement

- Product licensing

- Digital rights management

- GDPR data protection

- Managed services

Each of these areas will deliver efficiencies, resulting in a temporary increase in margins, offsetting early-stage implementation costs. Then, as the technology propagates, increased margins will erode and implementation costs will drop, leaving behind a more efficient system than its predecessor. Let's look at a few areas in more detail.

International Remittances

Africa leap-frogged over telephone landlines. Cell phone technology developed before most African countries installed physical telephone cables to all of their residents. As a result, they skipped right over that technology and went directly to cell phone towers instead. Landlines are much more expensive to install than cell phone towers, so they bypassed them entirely.

The same thing is happening with blockchain. One of the clearest use cases for cryptocurrencies like Bitcoin is for international remittances. Mexico receives about $25 billion each year (according to Banco de Mexico) from Mexican expats living and working in America who send money back home to their families. This is common when anyone from a developing country moves to and secures a job in a developed economy.

The standard of living is very different in developed economies than in less developed economies. A thousand US dollars goes a long way when converted to pesos in Mexico or rupees in India. That's why American tourists always look rich when they're traveling. They're not all rich, that's for sure, but they look rich because their money goes further in developing countries.

As a result, Mexicans who secure a job in America can easily send a few hundred dollars home each month. It doesn't affect them that much, but it makes a huge difference for the recipients in Mexico. In fact, international remittances make up a significant portion of GDP for many developing countries.

The Philippines are working on a blockchain-based system to allow their expats from around the world to send money back home without paying the exorbitant fees (sometimes as high as 10%) of Western Union, MoneyGram, and other similar companies. In so doing, they may leap-frog right over the traditional banking infrastructure that exists in developed economies.

For this analysis, let's assume the average fee for international remittances using traditional channels like Western Union is 8% of the total money transferred. Using Mexico for a convenient example, their incentive to develop blockchain infrastructure for remittances would be about $2 billion annually (8% of $25 billion). If they could bypass Western Union, they would bring another $2 billion into their economy each year. That's huge.

At the time of this writing, Mikmet Ersek is the CEO of Western Union. Do you think he sees the writing on the wall? Will their business model be wiped out by blockchain? Not surprisingly, Western Union has jumped on board themselves. They've already invested in blockchain and plan to improve their business with the new technology. MoneyGram has done the same thing.

Banks and insurance companies won't sit idly by as their businesses are stolen away by blockchain-based competitors. Instead, they'll lead the charge, attempting to protect their revenue streams from disruption. They may resist the new technologies on some levels, but they'll be actively embracing them on others.

Ripple is a cryptocurrency that's specifically designed for international remittances and cross-border payments between banks. Ripple's development has been endorsed by dozens of banks around the world, all hoping to profit from the new paradigm, and POCs and pilot programs have already been initiated to test the network.

International remittances introduce a counterintuitive variable to the normal technology adoption pattern. Developing economies have significant incentives to deploy the technology quickly. Their citizens (and, hence, their economies) could benefit the most. That means that blockchain technology may propagate faster in developing countries than in advanced economies. That's the opposite of most technology adoption patterns.

Disruptive innovation often caters to the least profitable market segment first. We'll be discussing this later in Section Five. For now, if you think about the least profitable market segment for financial transactions, you'll quickly focus on the poor and mostly unbanked citizens of developing countries.

This is a classic example of disruption in the making. Blockchain has the potential to bring banking services to people who have almost no money at all. If it gains traction in that arena, it could easily sweep through the entire global system thereafter. And if it came from that direction—from poor developing countries—it will certainly catch most American executives by surprise.

The developed world basically includes the USA, Canada, Europe, Israel, Japan, South Korea, Australia, and New Zealand. Technology normally starts there and spreads to other countries down the road. That's what's happening with artificial intelligence. And in many ways, it's happening with blockchain too, but there's a wildcard in the race. Consumer-facing (B2C) blockchain applications could easily propagate in developing countries first.

This is not a problem, but leaders need to anticipate possibilities like this. Always ask yourself how new technologies are likely to spread. We did a similar exercise when sorting your competitors by gross profit. The objective is the same. Success requires optimizing limited resources. Anticipating the path of new technology adoption is critical to that process.

Digital Payments

The digital payments space clearly includes international remittances, but there are far more applications as well. Bitcoin can already be used to purchase regular items such as a cup of coffee, a pair of boots, or a Tesla. The number of businesses accepting Bitcoin is increasing every day.

An interesting measure is the number of daily Bitcoin transactions. Back in 2009, there were generally less than 100 transactions per day. During 2013 and 2014, the number averaged between 50,000 and 100,000. In early 2018, it ranged between 350,000 and 400,000 transactions per day. Since all Bitcoin transactions are recorded on the blockchain, this information is easy to find. Simply search for "daily Bitcoin transactions" on Google and it'll come up immediately.

There's an important distinction between the number of daily transactions and the volume of those transactions measured in a different currency, such as USD for example. Because the value of Bitcoin has been increasing, the volume of transactions measured in USD has also been going up, even though the number of transactions has been relatively stable. When tracking Bitcoin adoption, make sure you're looking at daily transactions.

As long as the number of daily transactions continues to climb, the value of Bitcoin should continue to climb as well. Keep in mind that the total number of Bitcoins are limited to 21 million. There are currently about 16.5 million Bitcoins in circulation. With a finite supply, increased demand will translate into increased value. It's also a proxy for the broad adoption of Bitcoin as a payment method. As the number of transactions increases, it will increasingly make sense for other companies to start accepting Bitcoin as well.

Keep in mind that the speculative buying and selling of Bitcoin is included in the number of daily transactions. If you wanted to isolate the transactions where Bitcoin was actually used to transact commerce (buy a coffee, boots, or a car), you would have to deduct the transactions made strictly for trading or investment purposes. If that was done, you would quickly see that Bitcoin is generally not being used to transact commerce. Instead, it's being bought and sold by speculative investors, looking to profit from the hype.

Nevertheless, progress is being made. Japan passed legislation in early 2017 making Bitcoin (and virtual currencies in general) legal tender. Other countries such as Estonia, America, South Korea, and the Nordic countries including Denmark and Sweden are also embracing Bitcoin by passing legislation to accommodate it. It's inevitable that this legislative adoption will continue in countries around the world.

Does your company accept Bitcoin? Are there any other companies in your industry that accept Bitcoin? This is another area you need to be cognizant about. In these early stages, it's more of a marketing opportunity than a revenue opportunity. By accepting Bitcoin, you look progressive and tech-savvy, but incremental revenue will be limited. Over time, however, if adoption grows, the revenue opportunity will grow with it. Stay ahead of the curve. Start accepting Bitcoin today.

The opportunity goes beyond Bitcoin-denominated transactions as well. Blockchain allows payments to be processed without a central regulating authority. That disintermediation allows for micro payments, dramatically increasing the number of transactions worth processing. For example, people might donate tiny sums to content creators online or struggling artists they appreciate.

The technology can be used in a variety of other areas, some of which could transform parts of your business. Product licensing and digital rights management come to mind. These use cases are only beginning to emerge, but it's inevitable that more applications will be found.

Be proactive about this. Start building the infrastructure. Attend conferences in your industry and look for sessions on blockchain. Speak with your suppliers and customers to see if they're using the technology themselves.

Consider speaking with your competitors as well. They may be willing to share their thoughts, particularly with supply chain applications in mind.

Competing Cryptocurrencies

There are over a thousand different cryptocurrencies. Hundreds of companies have used initial coin offerings (ICOs) to raise money, each one introducing a new cryptocurrency in the process. It's a gold rush out there! The *State of the Token Market* report (compiled by Fabric Ventures and TokenData) estimates that startups raised over $5.6 billion in 2017 with ICOs. Leading coins including Bitcoin, Ethereum, Litecoin, Ripple, and Monero each attempt to solve different problems. Which ones will stay relevant? Which ones will fade away?

It's impossible to anticipate the success of one cryptocurrency over another, but it's safe to assume that Bitcoin and Ethereum will remain dominant. There are plenty of websites that track the market capitalization of different cryptocurrencies. Make a point to check back from time to time, staying updated on the market leaders. On the other hand, there are also some possible events that could wipe out the entire lot.

What would happen if a government decided to put their national currency on the blockchain? What would happen if the US government put the US dollar on the blockchain? It's the primary reserve currency all around the world. As mentioned above, the biggest problem with Bitcoin is that very few people are using it to actually transact commerce. Most are just buying and holding them as speculative investments. But an existing national currency is already being used, at least within that country's borders.

Singapore is working hard to do just that. They want to put their currency on the blockchain, releasing it from its border constraints and allowing it to be used by anyone anywhere around the world. There's no reason why other countries can't do the same thing. China is toying with the idea. Russia and Venezuela are both considering launching their own cryptocurrencies in order to circumvent international sanctions. These possibilities would all spell trouble for existing cryptocurrencies including Bitcoin itself.

It's worth mentioning that such nation-sponsored cryptocurrencies could conceivably be designed to record every single transaction within their economies, facilitating a level of surveillance never before seen in human history. National intelligence agencies including the NSA, FBI, and CIA would all *love* to have that level of visibility, surveillance, and control. Of course, if they were designed for such repressive purposes, they would meet fierce resistance from the public.

Puerto Rico has recently become a focal point in world of cryptocurrencies as well. After Hurricane Maria caused widespread infrastructure damage in September 2017, recently minted cryptocurrency millionaires and billionaires (including former child actor and cryptocurrency enthusiast, Brock Pierce, among others) saw an opportunity. The island needed help and they had a vision for a better tomorrow, not to mention the non-existent federal and state tax rates to protect their new wealth. Their goal is to create a crypto utopia where all money is virtual and all contracts are public. Local authorities are warming up to the idea.

The inevitable success or failure of cryptocurrencies rests with market adoption. In order for them to propagate, people need to use them to transact actual commerce. People need to get paid in them. They need to buy their groceries with them. They need to feel comfortable saving them in digital wallets, perhaps even with retirement savings in mind. The first cryptocurrency that achieves that level of adoption will win the race.

There are other specific applications that might favor different, more specialized cryptocurrencies. Once again, the supply-chain management use case comes to mind. Companies will likely create private blockchains to disintermediate their supply chain transactions, and Ethereum is well designed for this application. It's certainly possible that it could be used within the supply chain, even if a different coin has broader consumer adoption.

Sign up for a newsletter about blockchain developments. There are hundreds to choose from. Search for "blockchain newsletter" on Google. I receive a synopsis each Friday including the five hottest stories of the week. I can scroll through it in two or three minutes and always feel up-to-date on the latest developments.

Digital Identity

Digital identity is another important use case for blockchain technology. In healthcare, you've probably interacted with a variety of different companies and provided your contact details in each case. The same is true with banks and insurance companies. You probably have accounts and/or insurance policies with multiple companies, and you provided your information each time.

We all come face-to-face with this reality when we move. The process of updating your mailing address with everyone is cumbersome and tedious. It's also fraught with errors. Different companies have slightly different versions of your address. In my case, with a last name that includes thirteen letters and only three vowels, I receive a wide variety of spellings in my mailbox.

Blockchain technology can solve this problem. Imagine all of your contact details encrypted and stored on a public blockchain. When interacting with a new company, you could simply grant them access (with a public key) and always know that your information is accurate and up-to-date. For the companies, it would offer new administrative efficiencies and dramatically reduce error rates.

ID2020 is a public-private partnership (driven by Accenture on the Microsoft Azure platform) to provide recognized identity to over a billion mostly undocumented people around the world. Lack of identity deprives these people of basic rights, protections, and services. Many are refugees. Using ID2020, these people can use their phones to prove who they are and where they came from.

In 2016, India passed legislation granting funding for the Aadhaar program. It issues a 12-digit unique identity number (based on biometric and demographic data) to all Indian citizens, allowing the government to better deliver and track social service programs. As of this writing, Aadhaar has enrolled over 99% of citizens age eighteen or older. Although this biometric database is not on the blockchain, it represents a perfect model of what *could* be on the blockchain in the future.

The beauty of a blockchain-based identity ledger is that the identity holder—the customer—can use the same profile for numerous different purposes. Think about your own industry. Could it benefit from such a platform? Could you collaborate with your competitors to create it? Blockchain is coming either way, so you may as well be the disruptor, not the disrupted.

I recently spoke in Colombia to their stock exchange association. The attendees included representatives from Colombia's three largest banks, all domestically owned. I suggested they collaborate with each other to build a blockchain-based identity ledger. Between the three of them, they would definitely account for the majority of Colombian citizens. If the project gained traction, it could spread beyond Colombia's borders, perhaps spreading across Latin America.

Such an identity ledger would result in fewer errors and enhanced efficiency, but it would also allow these banks to tailor the specifications to work well with their existing systems. It would position them as progressive leaders instead of outdated followers. Tomorrow's economy favors progressive brands.

Initiate conversations with your competitors. Take the initiative and help build the future. Blockchain is an enabling technology to digital identity. We know it's coming. It's just a question of who takes the lead.

Land Ownership

Land ownership is a primary driver of economic development. Unfortunately, a huge number of property owners around the world have tainted titles on their land. In other words, their title is disputed. Most countries have centralized systems to maintain property ownership records, but those records include errors and competing claims on the same land.

Blockchain is a perfect solution for this. Since land ownership is a matter of public record already, it would be easy to move all of those records to a distributed ledger. A number of countries (including Sweden, Ukraine, Honduras, and Colombia among others) have already experimented with this approach. The tricky part, of course, would be to resolve title disputes before adding the information to the blockchain.

Here in America, when you purchase a home, you have to purchase title insurance as part of the transaction. That insurance is specifically designed to protect against tainted and/or disputed title. If land ownership records existed on a public blockchain, the title insurance industry would be wiped out entirely. An immutable record of land title with complete traceability would make title insurance unnecessary.

The title insurance industry generates annual revenues over $12 billion and employs many thousands of people across the country, not to mention the claims adjusters, appraisers, examiners, and investigators who operate in the same ecosystem. That industry will be disrupted as soon as someone begins the dirty work of creating the ledger in the first place. It won't be easy, but it's inevitable.

Similar applications have been used to follow precious stones such as diamonds from the original mine all the way to the retail customer. BlockVerify is a startup in this space. They also work with pharmaceuticals and luxury items. Other applications include the tracking of GMO (genetically modified organism) crops from fields to grocery stores. In all cases, the customer can easily trace items back to their original source along with all of the steps they took on their way to the final transaction.

Proof of ownership is a major use case for blockchain protocol. What assets in your industry are coveted by your customers? What inputs sometimes have questionable origins? What is commonly counterfeited in your industry? These are all things that might benefit from being on a distributed ledger. Speak with your competitors. There might be an opportunity to improve the system for everyone.

GDPR Regulatory Framework

The General Data Protection Regulation (GDPR) was drafted in 2016 by European authorities to strengthen data protections for individuals within the European Union. To date, it's the most stringent piece of legislation about data protection and privacy. And since the European Union is an enormous market (with a similar GDP to the United States), all global corporations are expected to adopt their guidelines across all of their IT systems.

Blockchain can play a role within this regulatory framework. Blockchain's distributed architecture, immutable record, and encryption characteristics make it well-suited

for data protections. However, there are certain requirements, namely the "right to be forgotten," that present
challenges. Once you're on the blockchain, you can't be
taken off. These problems have yet to be solved, but it's
fair to say that blockchain will play some role in GDPR
compliance efforts.

Every large corporation will be working on GDPR compliance in the near term. The legislation goes into effect
in 2018 and there's a lot of work to do. Any company
doing business in Europe will have to comply with their
regulations, most likely including yours.

If you're a consultant, determine your capabilities and
put a presentation together, including blockchain applications and use cases. This opportunity is immediate
and offers significant revenue opportunities for those
selling the shovels.

If you're not a consultant, you may want to speak with
a few. Get feedback from your information technology
(IT) team and see what options are best suited to your
situation. It will be important to update your systems
before the lawsuits start pouring in.

Contracts & Legal Documents

Whether you're employing blockchain protocol or not,
contracts and legal documents will increasingly be
hardcoded into smart contracts. It will be a big job to
make this transition for existing contract formats, but
the efficiencies will more than offset those investments
over time. Start thinking in an if-then framework. All
future contracts will include these types of contingency
clauses.

A simple example of this if-then framework is to authorize payment when certain conditions have been met. In the Texas to China cotton example above, payment was processed and ownership was transferred when the barcodes were scanned at the final destination. Not only can this expedite payment without requiring any human intervention, but it can force payment as long as all conditions have been met.

This could be particularly useful in insurance contracts. When predefined conditions are met, payment would be processed automatically and immediately. This could deliver significant efficiencies to the claims-processing function.

Another application is to register immutable date and time stamps on a blockchain, verifying ownership or contract milestones at given points in time. Date- and time-stamped hash codes could be smart contract conditions themselves, ensuring timelines are recorded in an indisputable way. Blockchain technology completely changes how contracts are written and what they're capable of doing.

Blockchain vs. Databases

Blockchain technology is, by definition, decentralized. The information is no longer in a single place. Instead, it resides on multiple nodes across a network. As with everything, that has both good and bad implications. The alternative is to maintain the information on a single database. Which is better?

Regardless of technological advancements, performance on a single database will always surpass performance across a network. The biggest issue in blockchain right now is latency. It takes a bit more time for information to propagate across a network then it does to update a single database. So if the application you're considering requires high-speed performance, a database is the best way to go.

Confidentiality is also better on a single database. You can protect it more easily. It's only in one place. You have more control. So again, if the application you're considering requires strict confidentiality, a database is worth considering.

On the other hand, blockchain is brilliant at disintermediation. That's precisely what it's designed to do. If you're attempting to shed intermediaries or administrative functions, blockchain is the better option.

Blockchain platforms are also incredibly robust. Not only are they impossible to hack, but there are, by definition, multiple versions of the ledger. If something catastrophic happened to one node, it's a completely redundant system and the bad node can easily be bypassed, if necessary. It could also be brought back up by simply syncing with another node. If your application requires a robust system, blockchain does the trick.

I'm sure you have ideas of the role blockchain might play in your industry. Dig into those ideas. Would they require a blockchain to deliver the intended benefits? Or would a simple database make more sense? It depends on the core deliverable.

It's worth mentioning that smart contracts are not only available on blockchain platforms. They're just as powerful in database systems. In fact, we've had smart contracts for decades. They used to be called "stored procedures," but they're exactly the same thing. You can leverage smart contracts in both database and blockchain environments.

The science of today is the technology of tomorrow.
Edward Teller

SECTION FIVE: ANARCHY
SUCCESS AMIDST ANARCHY
REQUIRES DEFIANT LEADERSHIP

In Section Three, we talked about the increasing division between rich and poor. We mentioned the social tension that emerges when some people earn a fortune while the majority struggle. We also identified demonetization as a precursor to anarchy. People in the lower-income brackets have to be self-sufficient for anarchy to take root. In Section Four, we talked about blockchain and its fundamentally decentralized architecture. Since anarchy is a decentralized social structure, blockchain will play an enabling role. Let's bring these realities together.

Decentralization & Anarchy

Any time you transition from a centralized structure to a decentralized structure, you give up a little bit of power along the way. If the information resides all in one place, you have full control. But if it's in multiple locations, you no longer have full control. You've lost some power. With blockchain, there's essentially a transaction taking place. You get efficiencies but you lose some control. There's a benefit and a cost.

This is one example of a much broader trend. As a society, we're shifting from centralized power structures to decentralized power structures. Technology is enabling much of it. As businesses innovate, they invariably provide more and more options to the customer. Customers can increasingly ask for whatever they want. They're getting more and more choices all the time.

Henry Ford famously said, "You can have any color you want as long as it's black." That was one extreme. The company had all the power. The customer either liked the product as is, or they didn't. They had no option to impact the offering.

Over the years, free-market capitalism and the competitive process have resulted in massive increases in productivity. Ford was once the only major car manufacturer. Today, there are many different brands all competing against each other. The customer used to have no choice at all. Today, they have more selection than they can handle.

Last month, a friend watched a woman return a DVD player at Costco that she had been using for seven years! They took it back and gave her a refund. That's insane. No company should have to accept that, but they do it anyway. It's all part of satisfying the customer, and that's the only thing that matters. Companies trip over each other, competing for the business, and the customer has all the power. It's a more decentralized marketplace.

The media industry is one of the best examples of a newly decentralized market structure. We used to have roughly a dozen major media outlets. Today, with the blogosphere flying high, social media platforms of every flavor, dynamic YouTubers and prolific podcasters, we literally have millions of media options to choose from. They all have their own followings and they all accuse the others of "fake news." The market used to be centralized. Today, it's completely decentralized. In fact, the media industry is in a state of anarchy already.

Remember, anarchy refers to a society that rejects power. It's a political philosophy that advocates self-governed societies based on voluntary institutions. In other words, there's no central governing authority that everyone respects. Instead, it's "every man for himself." The media environment has degenerated into anarchy.

The term *anarchy* has very negative connotations. People assume anarchy implies chaos, but that's not necessarily true. Instead, it suggests that the market participants reject any central authority. That implies a much more individualistic, tribal, and self-reliant society. All of the nationalistic movements around the world (including Brexit and Donald Trump's "America First" doctrine) are examples of this trend towards decentralization; this trend towards anarchy.

So decentralization implies anarchy, but anarchy does not necessarily imply chaos. The media environment is functioning. It might be confusing and hard to follow, but it functions. As consumers of that anarchist marketplace, we select the media outlets we like and reject the ones we don't. The result is a series of echo chambers where consumers only hear the views they already agree with and never hear competing views. It results in multiple competing realities, where each reality has a perfect internal logic system. There's no way to change anybody's mind in an anarchist system. You have to pick the reality you wish to function in and ignore the rest.

Look no further than today's polarized political climate. There are intelligent people on both sides (Republicans and Democrats), but they interpret reality from opposite perspectives. They're both 100% convinced that they're right and the other side is wrong. We always hear that our elections boil down to the undecided voters. That's because it's almost impossible to change anybody's mind. Republicans and Democrats live in parallel universes.

This dynamic will intensify in the future as a result of emerging "deep fake" technology. It's now possible to manipulate video to make it look like someone is saying things he/she never said. Examples are already on YouTube, showing George W. Bush's or Barack Obama's mouths and facial expressions being manipulated in real time, matching words being spoken by someone else.

Similar technologies allow you to superimpose one person's face onto a video of someone else. Clips have popped up with Nicolas Cage in a wide variety of movies that he never starred in. Search for "deep fakes" on YouTube. The process has also been used to put celebrity faces (including Scarlett Johansson, Maisie Williams, Taylor Swift, Aubrey Plaza and Gal Gadot among others) on porn star bodies in graphic sexual videos.

The algorithms need as few as 500 photographs or video clips of the impersonated face to render convincing fakes, so with photos and video footage readily available, celebrities, politicians and media personalities are the easiest targets. Of course, this technology is improving all the time. It won't be long before fake videos are indistinguishable from authentic ones.

The implications are daunting. Not only can fake videos be created to depict controversial and consequential events (imagine a video of Syrian President, Bashar al-Assad, privately admitting to chemical attacks, or North Korean Supreme Leader, Kim Jong-un, declaring war on South Korea), but wrongdoers can also claim fraud (and innocence) despite video evidence to the contrary.

Anarchy is characterized by tribalism and competing realities. Decentralization and surplus information leads to self-contained echo chambers. Everybody has a different version of "the truth" and everybody has ample evidence to prove that they're right and everybody else is wrong. Deep fake technology will amplify this trend. Leaders need to pick their chosen reality and disregard the rest.

Most industries will trend towards this model over time, and it all starts with decentralization. There are plenty of examples. We used to have centralized power production. Today, there are solar panels on millions of private rooftops around the world, with more on the way. That's decentralized power production, and it's already having huge impacts on local power utilities.

Hawaii is struggling with this right now. People with solar panels are paying almost nothing (depending on the weather and the number of PV panels they have) to the electric utility company. About 12% of Hawaiian homes have solar panels. Meanwhile, there are enormous fixed expenses to maintain the electric grid. If the utility allocates those fixed expenses over only non-solar customers, those homeowners cry foul. And if they allocate them to those with solar as well, those homeowners buy Tesla Powerwalls (large batteries designed for homes with PV panels) and disconnect from the power grid entirely. That makes the problem even worse.

That's the interesting thing about decentralization. *Every time you try to stop it, you end up accelerating the transition.* Attempts to restrict Bitcoin, for example, have resulted in *more* interest, not less. If a decentralized market structure is sustainable, *the trend is unstoppable.*

We used to have centralized taxi service. With Uber, we now have decentralized taxi service. We used to have centralized hotel service. With Airbnb, we now have decentralized hotel service. We used to have a centralized monetary system. With Bitcoin, we now have a decentralized monetary system.

Blockchain is a fundamentally decentralized structure. With every successful blockchain application, we're inching slightly more towards decentralization. That implies that those with power will see it diminish over time, including large companies, governments, churches, and authoritarian regimes. There may be short-term exceptions, but the long-term trend will distribute power to the masses.

Napster (founded in 1999) and BitTorrent (founded in 2004) were early examples of decentralized platforms. Both offered users the ability to share files (music or software) between themselves. Both were peer-to-peer networks with no central servers hosting the files being shared. These were profoundly decentralized business models that threatened existing power structures in their respective fields.

The open-source movement is a model worth following. That term was first coined in 1986, but it really started gaining traction about ten years later. Open source is a decentralized software development model that encourages open collaboration. People contribute under the GNU General Public License. Linux is an open-source platform. Apache is an open-source platform. Joomla, Drupal, and WordPress are all open-source platforms.

Imagine the intersection between decentralized business models and decentralized software development. Imagine an Uber without the company Uber. It would simply be an online platform connecting drivers with people who need a ride, but there would be no company in the middle collecting 20% of the revenue. There already is an open-source alternative to Uber (and Lyft) called LibreTaxi.

Imagine an Airbnb without the company Airbnb. Imagine a LinkedIn without the company LinkedIn. Imagine a Skype without the company Skype. Imagine Napster or BitTorrent without their respective company structures. Imagine a PayPal without the company PayPal. That's essentially what Bitcoin is! It's PayPal without the company PayPal. It's a decentralized peer-to-peer payment network with no central authority.

The Bill & Melinda Gates Foundation recently launched the Mojaloop platform. It's an open-source peer-to-peer payment network built on blockchain technology. It's designed to accept multiple different fiat and cryptocurrencies. Whether Mojaloop survives or some similar platform emerges, something similar will inevitably gain traction. When it does, it will likely start in developing countries, not on Madison Avenue.

If that traction spreads, it could impact the entire monetary system as we know it. What will happen to national borders if the currency is the same everywhere? How will governments collect taxes if income is anonymized through cryptography? How will the economy function without a central governing authority? These questions can only be answered by walking the path, and we're walking already!

The best way to anticipate the future is to identify leading sectors and follow developments there. The media environment might be the best leading sector thus far, but the open-source movement is close behind. How are things evolving in those environments? Who's thriving? Who's struggling? Identify success stories and imitate them in your own business.

Two models immediately come to mind. First, there are the technology infrastructure providers. I'm talking about the big players such as Google, Apple, Samsung, Amazon, and Facebook. They all provide tools that deliver more power to consumers. In other words, their technologies facilitate the transition from centralized to decentralized power structures.

Google delivers the world's knowledge to anyone who wants it. Apple and Samsung deliver mobile access to that knowledge. Amazon provides an ecommerce gateway between buyers and sellers. And Facebook allows people to connect with friends and family without spending a dime.

Meanwhile, these companies have become incredibly powerful as a result of their efforts. In fact, the technology infrastructure providers are an oligopoly in today's global ecosystem. Their technologies and algorithms impact billions of people every day. These companies are more powerful than most governments, so they're essentially bucking the trend. By delivering power to their customers, they've become powerful themselves.

How can you deliver more power to your customers? How can you facilitate the trend towards decentralization? Pursue any opportunity to put power in the hands of ordinary citizens. People have grown skeptical and even disdainful of large, powerful organizations. They don't like large companies or large government bureaucracies. If your business model transfers power from large organizations to individual people, it'll be well received in today's decentralized world.

Of course, China has its own group of technology oligarchs. Baidu, Tencent, Huawei, and Alibaba are just a few examples. In many ways (Tencent in particular), their technology companies are ahead of our own. In that sense, they're a leading sector worth watching. What are they introducing? What are their most popular products and services?

The second model that's succeeding in this decentralized environment is the "tribal leader." I'm referring to people who demonstrate their expertise in the public domain and gain loyal followings as a result. Seth Godin talks about building tribes. That's the foundation of modern marketing. *You can't take power. It has to be given to you!*

We live in an intimidating and confusing world. People *want* leaders to follow. They *need* leaders to follow. They're desperately looking for guidance. And as anarchy spreads, their need for guidance will only increase.

In an era of surplus information, moderate voices get drowned out. They disappear amidst the noise. Only extreme voices get heard. That's a major reason behind our increasingly polarized political and media environment. People end up in echo chambers where they hear only those voices they already agree with.

The same thing is happening in business. In an era of surplus everything, average products are drowned out. There's no compelling reason to pick them. Only the extreme products stand out from the crowd.

In tomorrow's decentralized economy, you have to be *extreme* at something. It doesn't really matter what, but it needs to be something. You can be the cheapest. You can be the fastest. You can be the most powerful or the most customizable. You can even be the most altruistic. Pick your area of expertise and promote it across all of your marketing channels.

Success amidst anarchy requires defiant leadership. It requires a confident and assertive strategy to improve the world in some way. Your strategy may not appeal to everyone, but those who *like* it will *love* it, and they will become your raving fans.

A business colleague was a supporter and organizer for Prop 8 in California, which attempted to block same-sex marriage in 2008. He asked me if he should include that on his LinkedIn profile. Yes, absolutely! Whether you agree with his opinion or not, it's still his opinion, and plenty of people agree with him. Those who *like* him will *love* him for it. Why? Because he's taking a stand.

Here's the reality: People who don't like you . . . don't like you! Period. Don't waste your time trying to change their minds. *Take a stand!* Run your business with passion and fervor, and then focus on those who identify with your approach. There are people in your target market who are more passionate about your mission than *you* are!

Decentralized Autonomous Organizations (DAO)

Blockchain protocol has ushered in a wave of new business concepts. Startups such as Ethereum, Backfeed, Steemit, ConsenSys, and Provenance are all facilitating unique use cases for blockchain technology, and each would alter the way businesses conduct business. As capabilities increase, more innovative business models will emerge. Standard operating procedures are shifting.

One of the new concepts is the idea of decentralized autonomous organizations (DAO). DAO businesses would host all of their operating procedures in the form of smart contracts on the blockchain, replacing management entirely. It's a reasonable concept. If we know how a particular business model should work, it should be possible to code all of the rules in an elaborate if-then protocol.

LibreTaxi, the open-source alternative to Uber, could be a model worth considering. Once the technology platform is built out, the rules of operating the day-to-day business are known. They could easily be coded into smart contracts and hosted on a blockchain. This model results in only two market participants: providers and consumers, nothing else. All management and administrative functions would be automated.

This DAO concept could be implemented in a progressive fashion. It could begin with the automation of 10% or 20% of managerial and administrative roles, but these percentages would increase over time as smart contracts are devised to handle increasingly complex tasks. The important thing is that the DAO would have no central governing authority. It would be an entirely collaborative platform.

This type of business structure involves a number of challenges. First, if it did not have legal recognition as a limited liability entity, participation in the business could come with unlimited liability. Second, since all of the code would be visible and easily accessed on the blockchain, known security vulnerabilities could be exploited by hackers until all the participants, through consensus, agree to bug-fixing initiatives.

We have a long way to go before DAO business structures gain traction, but the trend towards decentralized power structures increases the likelihood that these types of organizations will eventually be possible. And when they are, they'll immediately become part of the exploding gig economy.

Imagine a world where people can select and contribute to hundreds of different business models. They could search for any type of business they like, evaluate the different roles available, and select a job of their choosing.

Compensation would be performance-based, allowing each individual to fully control the income they receive.

YouTube is a good model to follow. Anyone can start a YouTube channel, covering whatever topics they like (within their terms of service, of course) and earn money from the advertisements on their videos. The business model is simple. YouTube sells the advertising and splits the revenue with the content creator. Everyone knows how it works. Anyone can do it.

Felix Kjellberg, who makes YouTube videos under the alias "PewDiePie," is estimated (by Swedish newspaper *Expressen*) to earn over $7 million per year (not to mention sponsorships), and there are countless others monetizing YouTube videos as well. Most of PewDiePie's early videos were of him playing video games! Ten years ago, nobody would've imagined that that was possible. Today, Felix Kjellberg is a global celebrity (although he's come under fire recently for making anti-Semitic statements, resulting in reduced exposure on YouTube).

There are popular YouTubers in every genre. Smosh and Jenna Marbles rose to fame on YouTube. Justin Bieber's career began on YouTube. As long as the content creator agrees to monetize their content, they all earn money from advertising. Even my own YouTube channel generates some revenue from advertising. It's an opportunity that's only limited by your creativity.

Amazon Mechanical Turk is another relevant model. That platform connect companies with a global on-demand workforce on a performance-based compensation model. Open source is a third example. Anyone can become a software developer and start contributing to the open source platforms he/she is most passionate about.

In the future, there will be hundreds or thousands of DAOs with a wide variety of "jobs" available. Some people would be better at certain tasks than others. Some would simply work harder. Some would voluntarily work part-time while others wouldn't work at all. In a fully collaborative DAO business structure, any form of contribution would be welcome, and the compensation system would reward those who contribute the most.

Since all of the DAO smart contracts would be publicly accessible on the blockchain, everyone (both contributors to the business as well as others who are completely unaffiliated) could see individual incomes for each contributor. Particularly successful contributors would gain recognition as top performers. As such, some may spin off and become personal development gurus, coaching and inspiring others who wish to earn more money themselves.

Many of these mechanisms already exist today. There are already plenty of personal development gurus who earned their stripes by being top performers earlier in their careers. Brian Buffini in the real estate industry is a case in point. And many of these gurus post their monthly income for all of their followers to see. Pat Flynn (Passive Income Blog) and John Lee Dumas (Entrepreneurs on Fire) come to mind. The only difference is that DAO businesses would be running on a completely automated platform.

It's the ultimate gig economy. People could pick their own jobs and let their performance determine their individual success or failure. Free-market forces would automatically allocate human talent according to capability and performance. Income transparency would clarify expectations in the labor markets, and anyone who wants to work would have a variety of options to choose from.

Supply and demand in the labor markets would determine compensation levels for different tasks. If compensation levels dropped too far, some people would stop working entirely. It wouldn't be worth it for them. But if too many people stopped working, or if a growing economy required more contributors, compensation would increase again, attracting people from the sidelines.

It will take time for something like this to emerge, but the trends are all pointing in this direction. These business structures might start as special interest groups or charitable projects. They might involve groups of activists trying to enact change. These would be simpler enterprises. We've already had some early case histories including Dash and The DAO. But over time, the technology will evolve along an exponential curve and support increasingly complex business models.

New business models will bring new employment opportunities. We'll never see a day when all organizations switch from the old format to the new simultaneously. Instead, the evolution will creep in, increasingly impacting one business after another. Just as the service sector crept into our economy over decades, these new decentralized business structures will creep in as well. But after ten or twenty years, our employment markets will look very different than they do today.

Disruptive Innovation

We're living in disruptive times. The exponential nature of technology drives much of that disruption. Peter Diamandis talks about the six Ds of exponential technologies.

1. Digitization

2. Deception

3. Disruption

4. Dematerialization

5. Demonetization

6. Democratization

Once a product or service (or business model) is digitized, the process begins, and it goes through a predictable series of steps as it develops. The Law of Diffusion of Innovations (early adopters, early majority, late majority, and laggards) models the same process from the consumer adoption perspective.

New technologies often evolve in the shadows. They're vastly inferior at the beginning, but they follow that exponential curve and eventually explode onto the market with enough momentum that it becomes difficult to catch up. Smart and successful executives are regularly caught off guard.

If the new technology is digital in nature, the cost immediately starts to drop. Digital assets can be copied and transmitted without any marginal cost, so it's only a matter of time before the technology becomes ubiquitous and cheap (dematerialized and demonetized). After that, it becomes democratized, when almost everyone can access and use it.

There are two different types of innovation: incremental and disruptive. Incremental innovation comes from the center of industries. Experts, developers, specialists, and scientists make incremental improvements, year after year, as they compete in their respective markets. Things improve, but the improvements are incremental in nature. And while incremental innovation is awesome in its own right, it's not what we're talking about here.

The second type of innovation is disruptive innovation. *Disruptive innovation invalidates existing business models.* It comes from outside industries. It comes from the fringe. It comes from what Peter Diamandis calls "adjacent markets."

Think about your largest suppliers. Who else do they sell to? Those are adjacent markets. Think about your primary customers. Who else do they buy from? Those are adjacent markets. Think about the value chain you're a part of. Who else contributes to that same value chain? Those are adjacent markets.

Apple disrupted the music business with iTunes and the iPod. Then, they disrupted the phone business with the iPhone and the App Store. And of course, Google disrupted the phone business as well with their Android operating system. Today, those all seem like forgone conclusions. But at the time, they were shocking announcements. Why? Because they were adjacent markets. They were related but also quite separate from their traditional markets.

Facebook disrupted the SMS space with Messenger. WhatsApp and Snapchat did the same thing. LinkedIn disrupted the recruiting business and Amazon disrupted the book business with their Kindle e-reader. Uber is disrupting the food delivery business with Uber Eats, and Amazon is doing the same thing in the grocery business with Amazon Fresh. Google and Tesla are disrupting the car business, and Google and Facebook are both trying to disrupt the ISP (internet service provider) business with balloons and solar-powered planes respectively. These are all adjacent markets.

Adjacent markets are where separate industries overlap with each other. If you draw a few circles that overlap in small places, disruptive innovation comes from those overlaps. They represent the sides or the edges of each industry, not the center. They represent the fringe. *Disruptive innovation often comes from seemingly unrelated markets.*

What's the cutting edge of nutritional supplements? It's in horseracing. That's where they test the latest supplements. It makes sense. If you have big money invested in a horse that's not quite good enough to win, you'll test anything to see if it'll work. That's where they originally tested creatine. That's where they saw the benefits of D3 and the impact of Zinc on testosterone levels. *Disruptive innovation comes from the fringe.*

What's the cutting edge of online marketing? It's in porn and online gambling. That's where they test the latest wire frames, tripwires, and conversion funnels. Remember those "deep fake" celebrity porn videos? That's disruptive innovation coming from the fringe. The information marketing industry is another example. The gurus selling expensive self-help programs are the first to test the newest launch sequences and marketing tactics.

Jeff Walker started his first online business (providing stock market advice) in 1996 and soon experimented with email marketing and content sequences to build trust with his followers. He was turning his marketing into an event, with predefined launch dates and limited time offers. It was cutting-edge marketing at that time. The strategy involved giving away valuable content over a few days, building trust along the way, and building excitement for a big product launch at the end of the sequence.

It worked like a charm, and he was soon coordinating launches for Internet celebrities including John Reese, Frank Kern, and Mike Filsaime. These types of Internet marketers were definitely at the fringe back then (2003, 2004, and 2005), but successful multi-million-dollar launches soon caught the eye of corporate America and Walker began consulting for Fortune 500 companies to implement the same strategies for them.

Walker eventually created the Product Launch Formula (PLF) and used his own strategies to launch the program to aspiring Internet marketers. Thousands have purchased his PLF program and it's helped generate over $400 million in sales in dozens of different markets. Jeff and his early customers were once the fringe. Today, their marketing tactics are standard operating procedures.

Think about your industry. Who represents the fringe in your market? Who are the crazy providers that nobody takes seriously? Keep an eye on those players. *Look past the crazy.* Ignore the crazy. Dig into their websites. What are they promoting? What's their most successful product or service? Could you tap into that market yourself? Could you sell something similar?

Tracking the fringe is a valuable exercise, but there are other options as well. As mentioned briefly in Section Four, *disruptive innovation generally caters to the least profitable market segment first.* This is another fascinating framework. Think about your industry, because this happens in every industry.

What's your least profitable market segment? Who are the customers you hate the most? Ugh! They're horrible! You can't make any profit on those customers. They have no money and no appreciation for the sophisticated products and services you offer.

We all know where the profit is. It's at the top of the product catalog. It's at the high end. In a free-market economy, businesses invariably focus on the premium products and services. That's where the money is. Everyone tries to upsell their customers to the more premium options. Across every single industry, there's this pervasive upward pressure in the sales process. Who gets left behind? The people at the bottom: the least profitable market segment.

Sooner or later, companies come along and target that underserved population with simpler and less-expensive alternatives. Many try. Most fail. But once in a while, an innovation comes along that meets the needs of those underserved customers, and it starts to gain traction. If it satisfies the least-profitable market segment, it'll sweep through the entire industry and knock the dominant players off their perches.

The important thing is that the innovation often comes from the bottom. It comes from the market segment that everyone else is ignoring. That's why executives get caught off guard. They're not looking down there. In fact, during the early stages, market leaders even welcome these new innovations, passing their least profitable customers off to someone else.

This has played out plenty of times in the past. In the early 1980s, Smith Corona was the world's leading typewriter company. They had the best typewriters on the market. About the same time, the Commodore 64 was released. The Smith Corona PWP 3200 was a vastly superior product for business applications, and they continued to innovate in the years ahead.

In 1985, Smith Corona invented electronic dictionaries. Two years later, they introduced grammar checkers. Another two years later, they invented laptop word processors and in 1994, they started producing personal digital assistants (PDAs). Smith Corona was on the cutting edge.

During the same period, personal computers continued to evolve. Initially, they were seen as only appealing to hobbyists and computer nerds—the least profitable market segment. In 1981, IBM launched their first personal computer, model #5150. Apple launched the Macintosh in 1984. Capabilities increased and costs came down. By the early 1990s, the typewriter business was being disrupted.

Word-processing software evolved at the same time. Computers soon had more capabilities than the best typewriters. In the mid-1990s, most professionals switched from the "reveal codes" WordPerfect 5.1 product to the WYSIWYG Microsoft Word product. Laptops started decreasing in price as well. And by 1995, Smith Corona was bankrupt.

The same thing happened with digital cameras. Believe it or not, Kodak was the first company to develop the digital camera. Steven Sasson was the man in charge of the project, but the final product was clunky and the resolution was horrible. It was vastly inferior to the market-leading SLR models. Kodak abandoned the project.

Over time, predictably, digital cameras became better and better, and smaller and smaller. Resolution was scaling. Capabilities were increasing. Eventually, the picture quality was just as good as analog photos. Today, digital cameras are included on every phone and analog photography is a thing of the past. Kodak declared bankruptcy in 2012.

Who was the largest retailer in the USA back in 1930? Any guesses? It was A&P. Remember them? In 1936, they had over 16,000 stores! The disruption in that industry wasn't a function of technology. Instead, it was a function of price. New big-box stores such as Kmart and Walmart started offering lower prices in large warehouse-style stores.

At the beginning, they were seen as uncultured, drab, and low class. Well-to-do people would never shop at Kmart or Walmart, but the least profitable market segment—the bargain hunters—loved them! We all know what happened. These big-box stores soon dominated the industry while independent retailers were seen as overpriced and inefficient. A&P declared bankruptcy in 2015.

The least-profitable market segment doesn't need all the fancy up-sells. They don't care about the exclusive reputations peddled by industry leaders. They want cheaper and simpler solutions. So what do your customers want? Can you develop simpler solutions that satisfy their needs?

Today, these big-box retail stores are being disrupted themselves by the online powerhouse, Amazon. They're fighting back, but the disruption process has already begun. As product delivery becomes better, faster, and cheaper, retail stores will lose revenue to online alternatives. It's already common for customers to visit brick-and-mortar stores, take pictures of the products they like, and then order them from Amazon for less money.

In all three of these situations, and countless others, the innovation gained traction with the least profitable market segment first. In all three situations, the innovation was an inferior product at first. And in all three situations, the industry giants were caught off guard when the innovation reached the tipping point.

This even happens with countries. Japan was seen as a low-quality producer back in the 1960s and 70s. Behind the scenes, they were improving year after year. In the 1980s, their affordable and high-quality Toyotas and Hondas stormed the North American market and caught Ford, GM, and Chrysler flat-footed. South Korea's Hyundai and Kia are doing the same thing today.

China is seen as a low-quality producer today as well. It will evolve the exact same way. Their quality continues to improve, and they're aggressively building business relationships all around the world. In particular, they've made major investments in Pakistan and a number of African countries. China is already a formidable global competitor, but their market share will grow further in the years ahead.

There are endless innovations being introduced to the least profitable market segment all the time. Most fail. There's certainly no need to fear every new innovation that comes along, but it makes sense to monitor what's happening in that bottom market segment. Watch for innovations that gain traction. Watch for innovations that get people excited. Watch for innovations that could invalidate your current business model.

Disruptive innovation invalidates existing business models. I did some work for a wire and cable company that supplies wiring for data centers. I spoke at an event with about 400 installation companies in the audience. These people bought wire and cable from the company, and then used it when installing servers at new data centers.

After the event, the company executives asked me how I thought disruptive innovation would affect their business. I said that the server manufacturers should build their servers like Lego blocks, allowing them to snap together quickly and easily, and eliminating the need for any wires at all.

If this happened one day, it would destroy that entire ecosystem. All of those installation companies would soon be out of business, and the wire and cable companies would be in jeopardy as well. In order to avoid that, they should proactively reach out to the server manufacturers and offer to collaborate on the new connection formats.

This type of innovation may or may not happen. I'm no expert in wire and cable. I'm sure there are benefits to the current model that I'm unfamiliar with, but they still need to consider these possibilities. What innovation would wipe out their entire industry? How can they contribute to the new simpler solution? What could wipe out *your* industry? What would invalidate *your* business model?

Defense Versus Offense

Most business executives learn about disruptive innovation and instinctively assume a defensive posture. Disruptive innovation is scary. They don't want someone to come along and eat their lunch. The logic is sound, but defense is the wrong approach!

Business executives need to stay on offense. Who else's lunch can we eat? That's the mindset you need to thrive in tomorrow's economy. Don't spend all of your time looking for threats. Allocate time regularly to look for opportunities as well.

See the forest for the trees! People get mired in the details and miss the big picture. Focusing exclusively on the threats of disruptive innovation is a small-minded exercise. Looking for opportunities is expansive. It's full of possibilities. It's exciting. Not only is it more fun, but it's also inspiring and motivating for the people on your team.

Keep asking yourself those questions. What are your adjacent markets? Make a list by looking both up and down the supply chain. Look at your own business model too. What's your least profitable market segment? What are those annoying and frugal customers looking for?

We do leadership training sessions with clients to cultivate this type of mindset. There are a number of exercises that can bring innovative ideas to the surface. The trick is to find the 15% of the population that instinctively embraces new ideas (we call them "movers"), and then hold back those who instinctively poke holes in new ideas. It's all about making your team feel safe when bringing new ideas to the surface, and heard when they have suggestions for improvement.

Strategic thinking and design thinking both require structure. We work with Allen Fahden and Karla Nelson, business trainers (and also personal friends) who've developed a model that categorizes people along the well-known Diffusion of Innovations curve (early adopters are "shakers," early majority are "movers," late majority are "provers," and laggards are "makers"). We all naturally fall into one of those categories, and it dramatically impacts the way we create, promote, implement, and address challenges with new ideas.

Most companies have good people on their payroll. The problem is that those people are often doing things they're not naturally good at. By aligning your people with the tasks that match their individual instincts, you can immediately increase innovative thinking without increasing your payroll. The results are always inspiring. Contact us if you would like more information about these training programs.

Pricing Strategy

The forgoing discussion is not to suggest that you need to focus exclusively on simple inexpensive solutions for your least favorite customers. There's enormous marketing potential by going premium. In fact, if you're in a B2C business, with the increasing division between rich and poor, you really can't go premium enough!

Monitor both extremes. Keep pushing premium solutions, but cultivate awareness at the bottom end as well. Schedule it. Allocate time to evaluate what's happening down in the dregs of your industry. That way, if disruption is brewing, you won't be caught off guard.

Cultivating awareness at the bottom is all about anticipating disruption and, perhaps, even creating disruption yourself. Can you reshape your industry from the bottom up? Can you reshape an adjacent industry? Can you reshape the future? Coach yourself, daily, to think more strategically. *Train yourself to be the catalyst of change, not the casualty of change.*

But within the context of your current market reality, pricing strategy warrants further discussion. Pricing strategy is a core element of your brand.

In social dynamics, people talk about a person's "frame." It's synonymous with a person's confidence. When two people interact with each other, the stronger frame wins. The person with the larger (more confident) frame ends up leading the interaction. He or she becomes the alpha in that particular setting.

The Law of State Transfer says that your emotional state will tend to transfer to the person you're speaking with. If you're excited, that excitement will transfer to the other person. If you're scared or skeptical, that will transfer too. Well, if you're the alpha in a social setting (i.e., you have the more confident frame), your emotional state will guide the interaction more than the other person's frame.

The best example of frame control in recent times was the social dynamics between Donald Trump and Jeb Bush. Whether you love Donald Trump or hate him, he simply had a more dominant frame than Jeb Bush. It wasn't even close. So any time they were standing beside each other, Jeb ended up looking meek and insecure.

We've all met people with enormous confidence, and it's difficult to match their energy. Growing up, our neighbor owned a large Chrysler dealership, and he was always very alpha, confident, and even arrogant. I always felt like I couldn't get a word in edgewise. He dominated every conversation we had.

Business interactions operate the same way. Businesses have confidence and businesses have insecurities. The trick is to project confidence into the marketplace and maintain it over time. It's called branding, and your pricing strategy plays a huge role in your brand.

Years ago, I worked with a company that manufactured wine jelly. At the time I met them, they sold little jars of jelly for about $4 each and also had a six-pack option for about $20. They were a retail shelf vendor, nothing more. There are dozens of other companies selling similar products. There was nothing distinguishing them from the sea of competitors.

I suggested they introduce an annual two-day ı
retreat in Napa. The first day could include a priv
tour of a fancy winery. The second day could include
workshop where participants could actually make wine
jelly themselves and take it home with them after. The
retreat could include three five-star meals each day with
every meal paired with different types of wine jelly. I
suggested a cost of $2,000 per person.

The key to this strategy is that it changes the frame of
the business. The previous business model was a retail
shelf vendor, nothing more. The new business model is
a hobby, a passion, a lifestyle, full of romance, culture,
and good food. It's a completely different frame. It's a
much larger frame. It's a more confident frame.

Here's the most important point: It didn't really matter
if anyone bought the retreat or not. The point was to
expand their marketing opportunity. They could plaster
this retreat all over their website homepage. They could
promote it in their email messages and advertising cam-
paigns. They could even reference it on the jar labels
themselves. It changes the frame of their business. And
if nobody actually signs up, well, nobody needs to know!

What's the most expensive product or service you sell?
Take that price and multiply it by ten. *What could you sell
at that higher price?* What would you have to include to
justify that 10x price? What about a 100x price option?
Could you create an all-inclusive premium option at
that price point?

Growing up, grocery stores carried wines in the $10
and $25 price ranges. But in the mid-1990s, they
started stocking $45 bottles as well. Very few people

,ttles, but it increases the sales in the
nat's pricing strategy. Nobody wants to
ͼ expensive option. But if you have $45
ͱe shelf, the $25 bottles suddenly look more

/ew premium option to your product and/or service
..enu. Add something expensive! It will change the frame
of your business. People will think differently about your
business than they do today. Remember, success amidst
anarchy requires defiant leadership.

If you already have premium options, go even higher.
Income inequality is increasing. The top end of our economy is literally exploding. Luxury brands are racing to
introduce ever-increasing premium options. Why can't
you do the same thing?

A friend of mine organizes 100+ events each year. A few
years ago, he started offering VIP tickets. They cost at
least 50% more than regular tickets, sometimes even
double, and include things like special seating, food
and/or drink credits, meet-and-greet opportunities with
speakers or special guests, and reserved parking. At least
a third of attendees pick the VIP option.

Another friend has a business selling premium foods
online (including foie gras, caviar, and truffle mush-
rooms). She introduced a luxury seven-day culinary
tourism trip to Italy. The first year, she only had six
or seven people sign up, but that didn't matter. She
promoted the heck out of that trip, and it changed the
frame of her business. She was no longer just an online
retailer. She became a gateway to premium foods and
luxury lifestyles.

Another friend runs a publishing co
duced the Nonfiction Author's Associ;
built a website online. People started j∟
she launched the Nonfiction Writers Conte.
online-only virtual conference, and invited speake.
contribute. People started to register and speakers were
happy to contribute. It was slow at first but grew each
year. Today, she has over 20,000 NFAA members and
they even offer book awards in the nonfiction book
category.

The association is booming. She's at the center of a
thriving community of nonfiction authors and, surprise, surprise, her publishing company is booming as
well. Imagine: NFAA offers book awards! The branding
couldn't be any better. Her frame beats the competition.
Her frame wins.

Imagine what the industry pioneer would do in your
industry. What type of products or services would the
industry leader provide? Can you be that industry pioneer? Can you introduce those premium packages? This
is precisely the type of leadership that works well in a
decentralized market environment. Take a stand! Offer
your customers premium options that aren't available
today.

The easiest way to go premium is to introduce a do-it-for-
you solution. In a world of surplus everything, companies
need to bring customers closer to their desired end result.
They can't just sell a promise. They need to sell solutions.
Ideally, they need to sell guaranteed results!

Give your customers a way to effectively outsource the
implementation of your product or service to *you*. Let

buy the final results, paying you to do all the heavy
lifting. That way, the value proposition is much more
compelling, and you control the implementation. Of
course, you're taking on more risk, and it's a lot more
work, but you can also charge a lot more money.

A friend sold a one-year license of his intellectual property to an industry supplier for $200,000. The problem
was that the supplier never leveraged the content prop-
erly. Many marketing opportunities were missed. Why?
Because people are busy. They just didn't have time to
leverage all the possible opportunities.

At the end of the year, discussions began to potentially
renew the contract. Knowing that they didn't obtain
much value, the supplier wanted a lower price to continue for a second year. Instead of lowering the price,
however, he included a do-it-for-you marketing plan
and actually *increased* the price! In other words, he leveraged his own content on their behalf, and charged
them handsomely for it. Was it a lot more work? Yes,
of course. Was he assuming more risk? Yes, but he now
had full control over the marketing process and could
deliver better outcomes, all while increasing his revenue
and profit.

How can you bring your customers closer to their desired
destination? Could you introduce a do-it-for-you solution that moves the implementation from their business
to yours? That would allow you to increase the pricing
structure and expand down the supply chain, an adjacent market.

Raise your prices. Introduce more premium options.
Always reference premium options in your marketing

communications. It will expand the frame of your business. It will improve your brand.

The MAYA Principle

Raymond Loewy (1893–1986) is often referred to as the father of Industrial Design, and his track record is impressive. Among many others, he designed the Coca-Cola bottle as well as the logos for Air Force One, Shell Oil, Greyhound, and the United States Postal Service (USPS). He had one guiding principle: design for the future, but deliver that future gradually.

The acronym MAYA stands for "most advanced yet acceptable," and it suggests that people like progressing towards the future, but only in a natural progression from the present. Loewy said, "The adult public's taste is not necessarily ready to accept the logical solutions to their requirements if the solution implies too vast a departure from what they have been conditioned into accepting as the norm."

You can see this concept play out in countless ways. Specific car models evolve every year, but they're still recognizable from earlier models. The Apple iPod went through a number of iterations where each successive model was simpler and sleeker than the previous editions, all while maintaining a similar look and feel. These are natural progressions. The customer is not required to accept an entirely new concept each time.

The converse is that the public rarely accepts a futuristic concept if it's a complete departure from current alternatives. If it's too big of a change, it generally fails. Google Glass is a notable example. The idea was good. Virtual and augmented reality are coming quickly, but Google Glass was just too big of a step for the public to accept.

Keep the MAYA principle in mind as you consider growth strategies for your company. Leverage all available technology to disrupt existing business models, but do so in familiar ways. Familiarity has value. It allows people to embrace the new without rejecting the old.

Chaos Theory

Chaos theory refers to a situation where the present predicts the future, but where an approximation of the present does not predict an approximation of the future. In other words, small differences in inputs have a large impact on outcomes. A common phrase is that a butterfly flapping its wings in Brazil can cause a hurricane in Texas. These are dynamic systems where tiny adjustments at the beginning cause a cascading domino effect, dramatically altering the trajectory and inevitable outcome.

When I was writing my fourth book, I had lunch with my literary agent and he asked me what my goal was for the book's eventual sales. To me, that was a naïve question. Obviously, I would've loved to sell 100,000+ copies, or even 1,000,000+ copies, but the trajectory would depend on the response to my early marketing efforts.

I had a marketing plan. That was under my control. The sales would depend on the response to my marketing. That response was *not* under my control. I had no idea if my marketing efforts would gain traction or not. As much as marketers try to anticipate the effectiveness of different tactics and strategies, the truth is that you never know until you test it.

John Wanamaker (1838–1922) was a successful American businessman and political figure, considered by some to be a pioneer in marketing. He was famous for saying, "Half the money I spend on advertising is wasted; the trouble is I don't know which half." Despite enormous advances in analytics, especially on online channels, this dilemma remains true today. Marketing attribution is extremely difficult.

I had a number of different mini-campaigns planned for my book, but I had no idea which of those strategies would gain traction, if any. If one was successful and others were not, I'd immediately shift resources towards the effective tactic and keep going. I'd continue spending money as long as sales were generated. And when all of my strategies were tapped out, I'd stop spending money.

My eventual book sales were 100% dependent on the response my marketing efforts generated. As it turned out, my approach worked for a while and I sold a few thousand copies, but it never hit the tipping point, and I backed off after about nine months.

The point is that you have control over what you do, but you do *not* have control over the response to what you do. Focus on the actions, not the outcomes. *You don't have control over outcomes. You only have control over actions.* This is true in all areas of life.

When you walk into a business networking event, commit to saying hello to at least ten people. You have control over that, but you have no control over the outcome of those conversations. Networking events are classic chaos theory environments. You could meet one person and the conversation could lead you in a direction you never would've anticipated at the beginning. Likewise, you could speak with ten people and end up with nothing. You just never know. The only thing you can do is focus on the inputs—saying hello to ten-plus people—and leave the rest to chance.

Let's assume there's a 10% probability that an attendee at the networking event can genuinely help you in some way. On average, speaking with ten-plus people should net you one productive conversation. Of course, you might get two or three sometimes and none other times, but the probability suggests one for every ten people you introduce yourself to ends up adding real value.

If you take this approach, two things happen. First, you improve and become more comfortable with the process. If you introduce yourself to ten people at a single event, you'll be better at it with the tenth person than you were with the first person. Humans are incredibly adaptable. We learn quickly. And if you improve, your "conversion rate" will increase in that activity. Over time, you'll achieve even better results; a higher conversion rate.

I discussed this in my TEDx Talk on "Learned Intuition." By immersing yourself in an activity (like introducing yourself to strangers), you'll quickly develop an intuition and comfort level with that task.

If you're trying to learn how to snowboard, you're much better off going five days in a row than going once a week for five weeks. In both cases, you're on the mountain for five days. But when you do it all at once, you're leveraging the power of your subconscious mind. Without even realizing it, you'll start noticing patterns and calibrating techniques. You'll adapt and learn. It's called *rapid skill acquisition,* and you're doing it every time you immerse yourself into something new.

Secondly, you'll end up with more opportunities in your life. If you introduce yourself to ten people while someone else says hello to just two, on average, you'll end up with five times more "lucky" connections and opportunities than that other person. *Luck and hard work are correlated.* The more action you take, the luckier you'll be. It's actually not luck at all. It's probability.

Take more action. Do more. Put yourself in more situations. One of my favorite sayings is: "The road to 'being' is through 'doing!'" If you want to be happy, do happy. If you want to be healthy, do healthy. And if you want to be successful, do successful. Do what successful people are doing, and do it a lot! Then, let probability take care of the rest.

In a world of increasing decentralization and anarchy, chaos theory rules the day. If everyone is defiantly independent, marching to their own drummer, the number of possible outcomes explodes. While more centralized structures with their predictable outcomes remain (work environments, church groups, political affiliations, etc.), we're clearly moving away from centralized structures and more towards decentralized alternatives.

Focus on the process, not the outcome. Build contingency plans, and be ready to pivot as you receive feedback from the marketplace. Tim Ferriss, author of *The 4-Hour Work Week* among other titles, talks about the minimum viable product (MVP). This is a response to the same underlying reality. Invest as little as possible to test your theory, and then test a lot of theories. If they work, invest more. If they fail, abandon them and move on.

In Silicon Valley, the mantra is to fail fast, fail cheap, and fail often. Test everything, and see what works. If you get some traction, iterate towards an improved version. Invest more money and keep testing. Keep going until the ROI dries up, and then analyze the project to see if there's another approach worth exploring. If not, walk away.

Social media operates this way too. When something goes viral, it can always be tracked back to one tweet or one share on Facebook, Snapchat, or Instagram, but you never recognize that magic tweet or share when it first happens. It's impossible to guarantee that domino effect ahead of time. Of course, there are things you can do to make it more likely, but it's never guaranteed.

I have over 700 videos on my YouTube channel. Sometimes, I record a video that I'm really proud of, and I expect it to do well once published. Other times, I record one that's weak and uninspiring, at least to me. The actual viewership numbers rarely line up with my expectations. You just never know. I have to focus on producing good quality videos—the process—and leave the viewership numbers to probability.

Test more. Try new things. Find the cheapest way to test new concepts, and then test every idea you come up with. You don't have to bet the farm on every possible innovation. Do it cheaply and iterate your way to success.

SECTION SIX: DEMOGRAPHICS
DEMOGRAPHICS DETERMINE ECONOMIC ACTIVITY AND ENTREPRENEURIALISM

This book is about anticipating the future and capitalizing on trends. We've discussed a number of frameworks already. The falling cost structure in data, the relationship between capabilities and innovation, the nature of disruptive innovation, and the trend from centralized to decentralized structures all give us glimpses of the future. But there are few measures as predictable and under-utilized as demographics.

When aggregated across entire populations, demographic trends are extremely reliable and accurate. If a baby is born today, we know how old she'll be in twenty years, fifty years, and eighty years. We know the probability that she'll die within the first five years of life, and if she survives those early years, we know how long she's likely to live. On top of that, birth rates per woman are also highly predictable, allowing us to forecast more than a generation into the future. The net result is a valuable and underutilized forecasting tool.

Demographic data is already heavily used in market segmentation and targeting, and its value is well established in that regard. Its potential as a long-term forecasting tool, however, is often overlooked. Meanwhile, long-term business planning (and, in particular, import/export expansion planning) benefits directly from demographic forecasting. Let's take a look.

The largest component of gross domestic product (GDP) is consumer spending. According to the World Bank, consumer spending in America represents about 71% of GDP. Most countries are between 55% and 75% (with a few exceptions including Russia at 39%, China at 34%, and Saudi Arabia at 30%). Consumer spending includes people buying food, clothing, shelter, energy, transportation, and entertainment.

Consumer spending is a function of the standard of living within the country's population. While it may vary dramatically from one family to another, across the entire population, it's quite predictable. So if you know how quickly the population is growing, you can predict how quickly consumer spending is likely to grow. And since it accounts for 55% to 75% of GDP, it's also reasonable to estimate GDP growth as a whole.

This isn't a perfect correlation, especially when population growth is very high, as in the third world where institutions are weak, corruption is rampant, and infrastructure is crumbling. In those settings, rapid population growth can reduce per capita income (i.e., the standard of living), offsetting expected growth. Even in these situations, however, overall GDP will usually grow, but at a slower rate than the population figures would suggest.

For countries with good institutions and infrastructure, the correlation is better, as in most first- and second-world nations. Most people are productive and earning money between the ages of twenty-five and sixty-five. Here in America, the average person reaches their peak spending year when they're forty-seven years old. Average spending by age is well documented by the Census Bureau. With all this data, you can refine the predictions even further.

The mapping of spending data by age is more important when you have variable birth rates. After World War II, birth rates shot up across North America, resulting in the Baby Boom generation. After that, Generation X (the children of the Quiet Generation) was 11% smaller and now, the Millennial Generation (the children of the Boomers) is 14% larger again. Those variations in generation size have already had significant impacts on GDP growth.

Harry Dent presented a simplistic version of this in his 1999 book *The Roaring 2000s.* His approach was simply to add forty-seven years to the birth data and base his predictions on that alone. Between 2001 and 2003, I built a model to calculate spending and saving data for every age in every single year between 1900 and 2100. Mathematically, the Baby-Boom adult spending cycle started in 1982 and ended in 2003. With the Boomers now retiring, it creates a drag on GDP, which hits its trough in 2027. After that, GDP growth should pick up again.

You can look at economies around the world and see this dynamic play out. Between 2010 and 2050, a forty-year period, Europe's population is projected to grow by just 1%. Birthrates are dropping like a stone. That's the primary reason why their economy is stagnant. Population growth is stagnant, and the standard of living is flat as well. That means consumer spending is flat. Unless net exports grow or the governments initiate debt-financed fiscal stimulus programs, GDP growth will be hard to come by.

America has higher birthrates, and our immigration has historically been higher as well. The result is a modestly growing population and modestly growing GDP. Mathematically, we'll continue to see anemic growth until 2027. After that, things should improve somewhat.

Obviously, these are long-term macroeconomic trends. There are plenty of other factors that add to the mix. The regular business cycle between growth and recession is a major factor in itself. Regulations, tax rates, and fiscal stimulus all make significant short-term impacts. Imports and exports can vary according to currency markets and trade policies. But over the long term, involving decades, not just years, the impact of demographics is unmistakable.

It's also important to acknowledge that population growth is admittedly bad for the planet, but it's great for the economy. The population can't grow forever. We're destroying the planet as it is, but the growing population is a primary driver of economic growth, and that's good for business.

Thankfully, birthrates are dropping all around the world. In fact, we'll actually end up with a population bust starting in about 100 years. It's already started in Europe and Japan. That's good for the planet, but a drop in population implies a drop in consumer spending, and that leads to economic contraction (recession) and higher unemployment. As with many topics in this book, there are both pros and cons.

We've seen the challenges of stagnant population growth in Europe and Japan over the past decade. Healthy democracies require healthy employment markets. If high unemployment persists, political opposition parties blame their governments, and voters vote for change. If a particular party wants to stay in power, the best thing they can do is reduce unemployment, and that requires growth.

Eventually, human societies will have to learn how to deal with economic stagnation and even decline. If the population tops out at eleven billion people and then drops back down to eight or nine billion, economic activity will grow and then contract in similar proportions. Democracies will have to navigate that population super-cycle, and it's likely to get ugly in the second half.

Europe and Japan are leading the way. They're both experiencing flat or contracting populations, and their economies are struggling as a result. Their economic experiments and political decisions are early case histories in the baby-bust eventuality. As low birthrates spread around the world, we will all learn from their experiences today.

Wealth Distribution

Thomas Piketty published *Capital in the Twenty-First Century* in 2014. It laid out a simple but powerful equation that defines how capital accumulates in different population environments. Basically, every country is evolving through three different scenarios.

1. First, women have five or six babies each, but only two survive the first few years of life. The net result is a stable population. One man and one woman get together and raise two children. That's replacement rate. We've had this for most of human history.

2. Second, women have five or six babies each, and most of them survive. That doubles (or more) the population every single generation. One man and one woman end up with, let's say, five children. That's massive population growth. From a global perspective, this started in the early 1900s and continues to this day.

3. Third, women have two babies each, and they both survive. This also results in a stable population, just like we had in scenario #1. This situation now exists in all developed countries and is spreading across the developing world as well. The notable exception is Africa, where birthrates are still very high.

In the interests of simplicity, you can think of the first scenario as the third world, the second scenario as the developing (second) world, and the third scenario as the developed (first) world. Also, keep in mind that falling birthrates today only affect the *adult* population numbers twenty years later when those babies grow up.

In the first scenario, the population has tons of kids and very few adults. In the second scenario, the number of kids per household starts to drop, the standard of living rises, and economic development advances. In the third scenario, the population is stable and the proportion of adults is much higher than before.

It takes roughly sixty years for a falling birthrate to transform the age profile across an entire population. That's a full life cycle for the babies born at the lower birthrate. This is closely correlated with the level of development in the country. Again, with simplicity in mind, you can think of the journey from third world to first world to take approximately sixty years, beginning when the birthrate starts falling. There are exceptions, of course, but it's remarkably accurate most of the time.

Keep in mind that a growing population and growing economy (assuming per capita income remains stable) lead to growing tax revenues for the government. For a country to emerge from the third world and eventually join the first world, significant investments are needed in public institutions and infrastructure. Governments who invest their growing tax revenues wisely develop much faster than those who squander it away.

Every country goes through this process at a different time. The process began first in Europe and spread to other then-developing countries around the world. It's fueled by the education of women, better healthcare, and more expensive childrearing requirements. It's too difficult and expensive to raise five or six children while holding down a job at the same time. Especially when women start working in large numbers, birthrates drop even further.

Falling birthrates also lead to increases in the standard of living. With fewer children in each household, parents have more disposable income and time flexibility. The best combination is a growing population (implying more opportunities and new wealth) and falling birthrates (implying a rising standard of living). Unfortunately, by definition, this is a temporary scenario.

Hans Rosling (1948–2017) brilliantly explained the planet's growing population amidst falling birthrates at the 2006 TED conference and returned multiple times for encore presentations. He was a Swedish physician and statistician with a talent for public speaking. He's brilliant, insightful, and entertaining. I highly recommend watching his TED Talks to better understand the relationship between birthrates and population growth. In *Capital in the Twenty-First Century,* Thomas Piketty discusses the simple mathematics that can be applied to all three scenarios.

When you have a growing population (scenario #2 above), you have new housing construction (to accommodate more people), new gas stations, new restaurants, new shopping malls, etc. These are all businesses, many started by entrepreneurs, providing products and services to the growing population. These businesses are earning a profit, creating new wealth. Meanwhile, at the end of life, the wealth of these entrepreneurs is split between five or six children, immediately diluting the wealth concentration.

This scenario creates a very egalitarian and opportunistic environment. New opportunities are everywhere and business success stories are common. Every time someone builds a new business and becomes successful, he/she becomes a role model for entrepreneurialism, and the accumulated wealth is automatically diluted as soon as it's passed to the next generation. America was in this phase for much of the twentieth century, resulting in mantras like "the land of opportunity" and "the American dream."

When you have a stagnant population (scenario #1 and #3 above), you do *not* have new housing projects. There are *not* many new gas stations or restaurants. Nobody is building new shopping malls. The existing gas stations, restaurants, and shops are enough to satisfy consumer demand. That means existing businesses earn profits, but it's difficult for new businesses to sprout up. In this scenario, at the end of life, the wealth of these business owners isn't diluted at all. It goes from the mother and father to their two children. The wealth remains concentrated in the hands of the owning class.

These two scenarios are characterized by increasing divisions between rich and poor. This was the situation during the industrial revolution (consider the bourgeoisie and proletariat in 18th-century Europe) and it's becoming the situation again today. It results in family dynasties like the Waltons and the Hiltons, the Koch brothers and the Mars family. Because birthrates are low, these families will retain their wealth for generations to come. Meanwhile, slower overall growth makes it difficult for new businesses to squeeze in.

Once birthrates fall, they don't go back up. If anything, they tend to drop even further. That means we're mathematically guaranteed to see the division between rich and poor widen.

The division between rich and poor fuels animosity and social tension within society. There's some fascinating research in this area. Monkeys, when given cucumber

147

slices for completing tasks, were content as long as they all received the same thing. But when some monkeys were given grapes, a superior reward, while others still received cucumbers, the disadvantaged monkeys became so angry that they threw the cucumbers back at the researchers. They were angry because their situation was no longer fair, and they could see it with their own eyes.

Poor people become angry when they have to coexist right beside rich people. It feels unfair. It reminds them of what they don't have themselves. The relativity is what makes it so frustrating. When everyone has a similar standard of living, it's easier. The competition fades away.

Planes that have first-class cabins are three times more likely to have disturbances in the economy cabin when compared to flights with only one cabin option like Southwest. For planes with two cabin options, those with doors in between the first-class cabin and the economy cabin do better because the economy passengers aren't forced to walk through the first-class cabin, reminding them of the disparity between the two. People don't like being reminded of how rich and successful *other* people are!

Income inequality pushes us towards anarchy.

I drive on the freeways in California and regularly see old beat-up cars driving right beside brand-new BMWs and Porsches. That's what drives people crazy. The division between rich and poor is too overt. It's too in-your-face. And with dropping birthrates, we're returning to a time when that division was even wider than it is today.

Of course, some people are motivated by that in-your-face wealth, fueling their own ambitions for success, but it only takes a minority of frustrated and angry people to raise social tensions for everyone. It only takes one riot to make the streets feel less safe. It only takes one mass shooting to instill fear in the population. Black Lives Matter and Occupy Wall Street are both manifestations of these social tensions. They're manifestations of inequality.

By combining the mathematical realities behind slow population growth and fast population growth with the relationship between population growth and GDP growth (via consumer spending), meaningful estimates of economic opportunities and entrepreneurialism can be made for countries all around the world. Let's look at a few now.

America

Modest population growth equals modest GDP growth, at least until 2027. The division between rich and poor will continue to widen, and the entrepreneurial mindset will wane. The visibility and in-your-face nature of American wealth will fuel increasing animosity within the working class.

Europe

Stagnant population growth equals stagnant GDP growth, and there's no end in sight. In fact, it's likely to get worse. Europe has a division between rich and poor as well, but it's significantly mitigated by their progressive tax structure and social safety net. This creates a more harmonious culture, but it also dampens innovation and entrepreneurialism.

Japan

Japan has the lowest birthrate in the world. Their demographic profile is catastrophic. John Mauldin of Mauldin Economics says that Japan's like a bug that's *looking* for a windshield!

Their population boom ended in the 1980s and they've been struggling ever since. The Japanese are very industrious people, and their economy is still the third largest in the world (after the USA and China), but they've lost the entrepreneurial horsepower in their economy, and their social safety net will have to be reduced eventually if they wish to avoid defaulting on their national debt.

Japan's national debt is the highest in the developed world as a percentage of GDP. Their people have historically been good savers, allowing the government to borrow from their own citizens, but that savings rate has evaporated in recent years, and their debt crisis is mathematically guaranteed to hit the wall at some point soon. When that happens, it will send shockwaves across the global financial system.

China

China's one-child policy is the primary reason behind their slowing growth in recent years. Their population is expected to top out before 2025 and will contract after that. China has recently abandoned their one-child policy, but birth rates remain below replacement rate.

China's big growth days are over. Also, the extreme nature of their division between rich and poor is stoking animosity there too, despite the government's attempts to suppress it.

On the other hand, the country's infrastructure investments as a percentage of GDP are the highest in the world, and that will fuel economic growth, productivity gains, and a rising standard of living for the foreseeable future. China will continue to grow but at a slower rate than the past three decades.

Russia

Russia's in a dire situation. The birthrate is below replacement rate and the life expectancy is only about seventy-one years. Alcohol consumption per capita is the highest in the world, except for three other countries also in the Russian sphere of influence, namely Belarus, Moldova, and Lithuania. Consumer spending only accounts for 39% of their GDP, so their alarming demographic situation won't necessarily destroy their economy, but it represents a significant drag on their growth potential.

Russia is one of the largest oil exporters in the world. The collapse of oil prices in 2014 hit the Russian economy hard, not to mention international sanctions arising from the conflict in eastern Ukraine and Crimea.

Their only other significant source of foreign currency is the sale of weapons. Similar to the stands at Costco where you can try food samples before buying, Russian involvement in Syria was essentially a live demo of their latest weapons technology, and it worked like a charm. Russian weapons sales have rarely been higher.

Keep in mind that Russia's economy is not very large. Their GDP is less than California's GDP. Yes, they're still a major geopolitical player on the world stage, but they'll have increasing problems on the home front and their influence will weaken in the years to come. The main concerns are their alliances with China and Iran, their sales of weapons around the world, and their stockpile of nuclear weapons from the cold war.

India

While India and China have been compared with each other for decades, they have handled their respective population explosions very differently. China invested heavily in infrastructure and forced co-ownership for all foreign investments, facilitating "technology transfer" along the way. China's autocratic political structure allowed for smart and efficient decisions, and their economy is much more developed as a result.

India is still plagued with massive corruption and crumbling infrastructure, but their best days are right in front of them. The population is growing at a healthy clip, and their economy is growing as well. Also, the one common language used throughout the country is English, making them perfect service partners for global enterprises.

This is an exciting time in India. Economic growth is creating that egalitarian environment full of inspiring success stories and new wealth. They're also undertaking ambitious projects (including the Aadhaar program described in Section Four) to position them for success in tomorrow's economy. The business horizon looks great for India.

Asia Pacific

It gets even better in the Asia Pacific region. The Asian Tigers including Thailand, Malaysia, the Philippines, and Indonesia all have growing populations with falling birthrates. The whole region is growing, including countries like Vietnam, Laos, and Cambodia. These are hard-working people with a scrappy, entrepreneurial mindset. They're a force to be reckoned with.

Of course, Australia and New Zealand will benefit from all this regional growth as well. In fact, real estate values have already skyrocketed in both countries, driven by rich Asian business owners who want fancy vacation homes in developed economies. Expect strong growth to continue across the Asia Pacific region.

The Middle East

The Persian Gulf region has been flooded with wealth ever since oil was discovered there in the first half of the 20th century. Knowing that oil won't last forever, these countries are investing heavily to diversify their economies. Dubai started developing in the 1980s and neighboring countries and emirates soon followed their lead.

The 2014 drop in oil prices accelerated the urgency of these efforts. Saudi Arabia, in particular, has announced a number of ambitious initiatives. The young heir apparent, Mohammad bin Salman (or "MBS"), has unveiled the "Vision 2030" blueprint to diversify the economy as well as the $500 billion NEOM project in the north of the country, along the Gulf of Aqaba, near Jordan, Israel, and Egypt.

Large development projects are also going up in Kuwait, Bahrain, Qatar, Dubai, Abu Dhabi, and Oman. These countries and emirates, along with Saudi Arabia, make up the Gulf Cooperation Council (GCC). Birthrates are dropping, infrastructure spending is off the charts, and they're literally surrounded with economic growth. Expect strong growth from the GCC region.

Iran

Iran sits on the east side of the Persian Gulf (referred to as the Arabian Gulf in the GCC region). They're also positioned for growth, albeit moderate growth. Birthrates are already quite low, and population growth is lower than neighboring countries, but the population is well educated, and they're emerging from decades of sanctions. Like the GCC region, they're surrounded with economic growth and have significant opportunities for development.

The problem with Iran is that they're the nemesis of Saudi Arabia and, by extension, the entire GCC region. Iran is a Shiite Muslim nation while the GCC countries as well as Turkey, Egypt, and many others are all Sunni Muslim nations. The two Muslim sects have been at odds with each other for centuries, and it won't end anytime soon. In addition, Iran doesn't recognize Israel's right to exist, and their nuclear ambitions have put them at odds with America as well.

If Iran can avoid overt confrontation with Israel, Saudi Arabia, or the United States, they'll enjoy respectable growth. The entire region, stretching from the Middle East all the way to the Asia Pacific, is primed for growth. Expect a collage of interesting alliances, coalitions, and partnerships across the Asian continent as different ideologies and religions compete with economic ambitions for growth and prosperity.

South America

Brazil's birthrate is lower than Sweden's birthrate. Chile's is even lower. While both of these countries have grown in recent years, their growth rates are dropping today. Other countries in South America, particularly Peru, Colombia, and Argentina, will fare better. Their birthrates are higher. Actually, Venezuela has the best prospects for growth based on birthrates, but their socialist experiment (introduced by Hugo Chavez and maintained by Nicolas Maduro) has destroyed any prospects for growth in the near term. Expect moderate growth in South America overall.

Superstars

I am often asked which countries I think are best positioned for success in the years to come. For demographic as well as geographic reasons, I think Mexico and Turkey hold the most promise for economic growth and regional influence. Both have excellent age profiles and both have favorable geography. Turkey connects the fully-developed European Union with the exploding Middle East region. Mexico has oceans on both sides and the world's economic King Kong on its northern border. Meanwhile, both have growing populations and falling birthrates, implying rising standards of living in the years ahead.

Volatility

Which countries will encounter the most volatility? Sadly, most of the sub-Saharan countries in Africa fall into this category. Birthrates are still very high and are only starting to show signs of dropping. Yes, these economies will grow, but institutions are scarce, corruption is rampant, and infrastructure is limited.

Populations that are composed predominantly of young people have higher unemployment. These young people aren't contributing significantly to GDP yet, and their parents are much fewer in numbers. That means the economy is too small to employ everyone, so the youth are generally underemployed, bored, and financially frustrated.

The people most likely to protest and cause trouble are fifteen- to twenty-five-year-old males. If a society has a lot of people in that category, and they're underemployed and bored, it generally translates into volatility and social unrest.

America had a baby boom too, and that explosion of young people translated into volatility and social unrest in the late 1960s and early 70s. The Baby Boomers were in their late teens and early twenties at that time. Today, most of Africa is in a perpetual baby boom situation. The entire continent is bursting with underemployed young people. That spells trouble.

Terrorism is directly impacted by these demographics. These underemployed young males lash out at the source of their perceived injustice. In America during the 1960s and 70s, that perceived injustice came from the civil rights struggle and the Vietnam War effort. For the past twenty years, high birthrates have been concentrated in the Muslim world and the source of their perceived injustice is Israel, the United States, and other western democracies.

The future of terrorism will increasingly shift from the Middle East to Africa. As birthrates drop across the Middle East, populations will moderate. Adults are a moderating influence on societies. Children will generally be more open-minded than their parents, causing a generational liberalization in political and social values.

It'll take at least another ten or twenty years for birthrates to drop in Africa and then another twenty years for those babies to become adults. Expect social unrest, terrorism, and chaos in Africa for at least the next thirty years.

In the Middle East and south Asia, a few problem spots remain. Pakistan's birthrates are still quite high (although dropping slightly since 2010) and volatility remains high as well. China has made major investments into the country, and that will certainly help, but we can expect at least another fifteen years of social and political volatility in Pakistan.

The only other countries in south Asia with stubbornly high birthrates are Iraq and Syria. With the conflict ongoing, sadly, these countries will struggle for years to come. A lot of people automatically assume that Afghanistan should be on that list too. Yes, there are still plenty of problems in Afghanistan but birthrates are starting to drop and there are some hopeful signs of progress.

The economic development laggards are almost entirely in Africa. That will be the epicenter of social and political volatility for the foreseeable future. Charitable foundations and foreign aid programs need to focus on birth control, educating women, and battling corruption. With any luck, birthrates will start dropping in the next decade or so.

Having said that, if you have contacts and/or opportunities you can tap into in Africa, the profit potential is significant. The population is exploding, so those economies will definitely grow. They'll grow quickly! It'll be a wild ride, that's all. Be prepared for corruption, bribes, unreliable partners, and dysfunctional institutions. If you can handle all that, huge profits could be your reward.

Africa has lots of problems, each one representing another business opportunity. Learn to look at problems differently. Problems all constitute business opportunities. So while Africa struggles with social and political instability, poverty, and corruption, it's a land of opportunity for enterprising business executives.

Globalization

This type of information allows for strategic decisions, especially if your company is in the export business. Which countries should you enter first, and in what order? Where should you open your next distribution facility? Where can you expect volatility and social unrest? You can answer all of these questions with an evaluation of their demographic circumstances.

Globalization will continue, regardless of the political rhetoric we see on TV. We're all increasingly global citizens, using technology platforms that render national borders meaningless. Decentralization is accelerating the trend. International trade will continue to grow. Tomorrow's leaders need to leverage that trend wherever possible.

What is happening with automation and globalization, that's not going away.

Campbell Brown

CONCLUSION
CHANGE CREATES OPPORTUNITY

Technology trends including artificial intelligence and blockchain provide ample opportunities for profit, even when macroeconomic growth is stagnant. Disruptive innovation will spell disaster for some but profit for others.

The average lifespan of a company on the S&P 500 index was over sixty years in the 1950s, according to Innosight. Today, it's less than twenty years, and that number will drop further in the years ahead. A study from the John M. Olin School of Business (Washington University) estimates that 40% of today's Fortune 500 companies on the S&P 500 will no longer exist in ten years. That means new companies will emerge to take their place.

Having said that, however, the opportunity is even greater when the entire pie is growing. It's easier to succeed when the economy is booming. Don't ignore the demographics. They can help you spot growth opportunities years in advance. What can you sell in Mexico or South America? What can you sell in the GCC region, Iran, or India? What can you sell in Indonesia, Thailand, or the Philippines?

When I started speaking full time, I quickly noticed that international conference organizers treated me differently—they treated me better—because I'm an American from Silicon Valley. That's nothing special here at home. But in Sweden, Dubai, or Bangkok, it makes me more competitive as a potential keynote speaker. Regardless of our political reputation these days, America still has a huge cultural influence around the world. You might be surprised how well you could do in international markets.

It's time to combine technology trends with demographic trends. How could you leverage artificial intelligence in India? How could you leverage blockchain in Malaysia? If you're up for the challenge, how could you bring disruptive innovation to Africa? They're the least profitable market segment and they have plenty of problems that need solving.

China has already made huge investments in Africa. Why do you think they're doing that? They see the opportunity. They're jockeying for position in a volatile region that's growing quickly. Can you do the same thing?

This is like buying a stock before the rally. We know that growth is coming, not only in Africa but also in the GCC, India, and the Asia Pacific region. The sooner you can establish a foothold in those markets, the sooner you'll be able to tap into that growth.

Aligning Incentives

The trick is to align everyone's incentives so they're all pointing in the same direction: the direction you want to go. Any business involves a number of different parties including producers, distributors, retailers, customers, regulatory agencies, and tax authorities. Map out all of the players in your industry and describe the incentive structure for each one. It's quite common for some of those players to have conflicting incentives.

Foreign aid programs are a good example. In response to humanitarian crises, charitable organizations often deliver food to the local population: rice, for example. But as soon as it arrives, it becomes impossible for local rice producers to sell their harvest. Why? Because the foreign rice is free! So all of a sudden, their local rice industry collapses.

Of course, at the time of the initial deliveries, the food is desperately needed. The foreign aid is delivered with perfectly altruistic intentions, but there needs to be a balance. As soon as the local producers get back on their feet, the aid should be reduced, allowing those local producers to fill in the gap. They are contributors to the domestic economy. Not only do they produce food, but they employ local workers as well. These businesses need to succeed for the economy to rebound after the crisis.

During the British rule of colonial India, there was a problem in the capital, New Delhi: too many cobra snakes. The British government began offering a reward for cobras that had been captured and killed by hunters. At the beginning, the program was a success with large numbers of snakes killed. Over time, however, enterprising people started breeding cobras, then killing them and submitting them for reward money.

When the British government discovered the racket, they immediately cancelled the program. Not surprisingly, the cobra breeders then released their now-worthless snakes from their cages. The net result was that the snake population actually increased from the original baseline. *The law of unintended consequences is rooted in conflicting incentives.*

People act in their own best interests. Put yourself in the shoes of your suppliers, distributors, channel partner, and customers. What would *their* best-case scenario look like? Get creative. What would a scrappy entrepreneur do in their situation? When incentives are all nicely aligned, business growth potential explodes.

The most important word in Silicon Valley is *scale.* Can the business grow exponentially? There has never been a time when business ideas can spread as quickly as they do today. The WhatsApp example from the beginning of this book is a great example. That platform now has over 1.3 billion monthly active users! Aligning all the incentives might be the most important requirement for your business to start scaling.

Surplus Capital

A large part of any business's success is the availability of investment capital at the beginning. There's good news there too. There has never been more capital available for business startups. Between individual angel investors, venture capital firms, private equity funds, sovereign wealth funds, traditional banks, and the bond markets, money is available around every corner.

There are over 2,000 billionaires on this planet, and that number grows almost every year. These are all people who have amassed enormous wealth from business ventures. As the global GDP continues to grow, countless more will enter their ranks. All of these people are looking for places to invest their money. They're all looking for a place to park their cash.

There's a growing pool of capital around the world. That's the reason we see these bubbles emerge in one field after another (the dotcom bubble, real estate, technology, Bitcoin, etc.). Although it's counterintuitive for some, we actually have a liquidity problem right now. We have surplus capital. All of that wealth follows the hottest new trends, sometimes inflating valuations beyond what's justifiable.

Interest rates will remain reasonably low for a long time. Yes, the Fed has been raising rates recently, but they're still within a historically low range. Besides, the borrowing activity affected by the Fed's published rate is actually quite small. Most of the trading activity on the bond markets involves governments and corporations buying and selling bonds, and those interest rates fluctuate as a result of supply and demand.

Interest rates in the bond market have been dropping for over thirty years. Yes, there are highs and lows along the way, but the overall trend has been down for decades. The reason is that we have more supply of capital than demand, and that will continue into the future. The growing number of billionaires is just one measure among many that reflect that fact. That means money is cheap and available for business ventures.

Of course, there's an elephant in the room, and that's the role central banks have played with quantitative easing. Over the past decade, they've pumped trillions of dollars into the economy by purchasing government bonds with freshly minted cash. Those stimulus programs have now ended and central banks are reducing their balance sheets.

Reduced demand in the bond markets will increase interest rates in the near term, but they'll still remain low by historical standards. We won't be seeing the 18% interest rates of the early 1980s, that's for sure. I would expect US 30-year bond yields between 2.5% and 5% for the foreseeable future. In fact, I'd be surprised if they ever rose above 5% again.

Crowdfunding is another source of financing that's emerged in recent years, including platforms such as Kickstarter, GoFundMe and Indiegogo. The Pebble smartwatch, Ouya game console, PonoMusic, and Oculus Rift are all well-known examples of business ideas financed on crowdfunding platforms, and there are countless others.

Last but not least, as mentioned in Section Four, the new market for ICOs (initial coin offerings) has delivered billions to startups in the past few years. While the insane ICO gold rush may already be behind us (peaking in mid-2017), this new funding channel will continue to evolve in the years ahead.

The good news is that money is always available for good business ideas. Likewise, business expansions based on sound principles are easily financed. This is the perfect time to take a leadership role and transform your business for tomorrow's economy. There are so many ways we can anticipate the future, and most of those trends are pointing in exciting directions.

It's true that the world is becoming more decentralized. It's true that anarchy is taking root, and the world will certainly change as that ideology permeates our global culture. But there are opportunities within decentralized ecosystems. There are opportunities for leadership and vision. There are opportunities for profit.

Think Bigger!

The message of this book is to think bigger. *Think bigger about what's possible.* I study visionary leaders including Steve Jobs, Bill Gates, Elon Musk, and Jeff Bezos, and their approach has predictable consequences. There's plenty of research on this. When you think bigger, you can count on some reliable outcomes.

For starters, you inspire everyone around you. People want to be part of the excitement. They want to be where the action is! And when you think bigger, people are naturally attracted to that vision. Your employees are inspired when you're shooting for bigger goals. Your customers are inspired as well. Even your competitors are inspired when you're thinking bigger!

People want to make a difference. They want to change the world. It's a natural human instinct. *Momentum trumps everything.* People want to be part of the action. Thinking bigger automatically triggers this reaction, particularly in a decentralized environment. The best way to engage people (such as your employees and your customers) is to take a stand and do something big.

Secondly, when you're thinking way bigger, quite often, you have almost no competition, because most people don't have the courage to chase those ambitious goals. Success is much more likely if you're not competing against anyone. And the easiest way to be in that situation is to do something bigger than anyone else is attempting.

Many business leaders are known for this type of thinking. Richard Branson is a great example. He also has dozens of great quotes. Here's my favorite Richard Branson quote: "The fastest way to become a *millionaire* is to start out as a *billionaire*, and then start an airline!" Brilliant.

Richard Branson started Virgin Galactic. You can't get much bigger than that! Does he have any competition? Not much! There are a few companies trying to do similar things, but he's mostly on his own.

What about Elon Musk? He's like a personal hero to me. I love the way he thinks. He thinks in first principles, meaning he boils things down to the most fundamental truths and then reasons up from there. It's a fascinating alternative to the analogy-based thinking patterns most others use.

Elon Musk founded SpaceX, the first private corporation to deliver cargo to the International Space Station (ISS). No private company has ever done that before, and they're reusing their rockets! They're sending the rocket up and then bringing the first (and largest) stage back down, landing it on a barge out in the Atlantic Ocean.

This is a perfect example of thinking in first principles. The cost of sending a rocket to the ISS is about $60 million. The exact amount depends on the cargo, but it's roughly $60 million. What does the fuel cost? Someone asked me this two years ago. I guessed between $10 million and $20 million.

The right answer is just $200,000! That's about one-300th of the total cost! So if you can reuse the hardware (the rockets themselves), you could bring down the cost function by 100-fold or more.

That's thinking in first principles. That thought process goes right down to the raw material cost of inputs. Musk likens the previous approach to throwing away planes after just one flight. That would be insane, but that's exactly what most space organizations do. They throw away the hardware (the rockets) after every launch.

Elon Musk saw those inefficiencies right from the start. He knew that reusable rockets were essential to bring the cost structure down, so he and his team developed the means to land the first stage back on Earth.

The first time they pulled it off was on December 21, 2015, and their employees partied like it was 1999! The average age of SpaceX employees is twenty-seven. That makes them Millennials. Millennials get a bad rap. People accuse them of being lazy, apathetic, and entitled. It's not true. Those Millennials will work harder than anyone you've ever seen if you give them something inspiring to work towards.

People get excited when you think bigger. It's not just a cliché. It actually works that way! When you're doing something big, your employees (including Millennials) get fired up and engaged in the process. Obviously, we don't all have the option of building rockets designed to fly to Mars, but we all have the option to think bigger about the projects we're chasing.

Does SpaceX have any competition? Not much! Yes, there are a few companies in the game, but very few. SpaceX is running the table. Blue Origin (founded by Jeff Bezos) is experimenting with reusing their rockets, but that's about it. That's why SpaceX has managed to secure such large contracts from NASA.

Elon Musk also founded Tesla. Any competition there? Not much, at least not when they originally launched. Nobody thought to produce a high-performance electric car. They only wanted to produce slow, ugly electric cars! Tesla took the challenge and gave their customers what *they* wanted.

Tesla released their Model 3 in 2016 and racked up over 400,000 reservations, more than any car launch in history. People get excited about visionary goals. It's true. Thinking bigger inspires everyone. Tesla is proving that every single day.

They also introduced their Powerwall, essentially an attractive battery that looks like a piece of art. It hangs on your wall, attaches to the solar panels on your roof, allowing it to charge during the day, so you can power your home at night, and disconnect from the power grid entirely! Any competition? Nope. None.

Tesla is currently building the Gigafactory in Nevada. Once complete, it'll be the largest building in the world by footprint. The Gigafactory will more than double the global production capacity of lithium ion batteries. Any competition? Nothing even close.

In the end, this book isn't really about technology trends or disruptive innovation. It's not about artificial intelligence or blockchain. It's not even about anarchy. This book is about vision and leadership. It's about staying on the right side of the leverage equation. It's about thinking way bigger.

All of these success stories are the same. These leaders all think the same way. They think bigger than everyone else, inspiring everyone around them and encountering almost no competition along the way. Steve Jobs did this throughout his entire career. He was always willing to do the big thing. He was the one who did it right. He's the one who anticipated the future.

This is an incredible time. Things are changing quickly, and elements of anarchy are coming. There will be winners and losers. Some will thrive while the majority struggle. Will you be among the winners? Are you willing to see the forest for the trees? Are you able to see the big picture? This is a time for leadership. *This is a time for you!*

Book Reviews

Please review this book on Amazon. Whether you think it deserves five stars, one star, or something in between, reviews are extremely important. We hope you have found value in the book and hope you'll share your thoughts for future readers to see.

Bulk Book Orders

Discounts are available for bulk book orders. Contact us if you're interested in purchasing this book for your team. Available formats include both paperback and hardcover, and custom messages can be included with larger quantities.

Media Interviews

Are you a journalist, TV show host, YouTuber, podcaster, or blogger? Patrick Schwerdtfeger is available for media interviews and special events. Contact us to discuss your target audience and content objectives.

Keynote Speaking

Patrick Schwerdtfeger speaks at dozens of corporate events each year. His primary topics include (1) Anarchy, (2) Disruptive Innovation, (3) Big Data, (4) Artificial Intelligence, and (5) Blockchain. Contact us to check availability and pricing.

Innovation Training

Do you need to cultivate a culture of innovation within your team? We facilitate online and offline training to harness innovative potential within your organization, both now and reliably into the future. Contact us for details.

Contact Information

The easiest way to contact the author is through his primary website:

https://www.patrickschwerdtfeger.com